Civilization As Divine Superman

A Superorganic Philosophy of History

Alexander Raven Thomson

Civilization As Divine Superman

A Superorganic Philosophy of History

Alexander Raven Thomson

ISBN-13: 978-1-913176-02-0

Sanctuary Press Ltd
71-75 Shelton Street
Covent Garden
London
WC2H 9JQ

www.sanctuarypress.com
Email: info@sanctuarypress.com

Dedicated to

Lisbeth Röntgen

In recognition of her loyalty and self-sacrifice
which have made publication possible.

Alexander Raven Thomson

Contents

Preface

This attempt to build up a systematic philosophy of history began with an investigation of those revolutionary changes of social structure, such as the Reformation and the French Revolution, which so obviously transcend all individual human agency. It was only after discovering that these social revolutions follow one another in rhythmic sequence that the writer developed the conception of a superorganic agency, supported by the similar conclusions of the German philosopher Oswald Spengler. He wishes to point out, however, that his superorganic philosophy goes very much farther than Spenglerism, embracing as it does the whole scheme of world history, while Spengler exalts only certain cultural epochs above the general 'fellahin' level.

The conception of religion as an unconscious veneration of the cultural superorganism has, of course, some resemblance to H. G. Wells's *God, the Invisible King*, but the writer asserts that the superorganic explanation of religion is much more in accordance with the many different religions of mankind and the ever-changing forms of religious faith. There is in actual fact no static spiritual belief in one great god of mankind, but several dynamic religions venerating separate deities of only local potency. Each cultural community is true to its own religion and its own godhead, and the proselytizing zeal of the missionaries is rightly to be condemned, as turning the native from his own true faith to the strange god of the foreigner.

No attempt has been made in this discussion to follow the tempting paths of prophecy that open, where the inexorable present shuts off all further investigation of the development of modern civilizations. Historical analogy would enable us to make many interesting suggestions of the probable further development of modern America, India, China, and last but not least of our own Europe. If there is any truth in the cyclic nature of superorganic development, it must at least throw a valuable light on what we are to expect from the future, but we must leave this enthralling speculation for a future occasion.

Alexander Raven

1

Introduction

Integration: The Metaphysical Basis

The modern development of experimental science has brought a wonderful confirmation of the early metaphysical conception known as 'monism,' which propounds the theory that all bodies are formed of one primitive substance. It has become within recent years more and more evident that matter as a concrete continuous entity is no more than an illusion, that all the various phenomena we associate with matter are caused by the action of various forms of energy.[1]

The Law of Relativity actually contains a formula by means of which mass may be stated in terms of energy, so that it seems that matter is no more than energy in a more concentrated form. The 'conservation of mass,' formerly one of the established 'laws' of physics, shaken by the discovery of radium and abandoned in the cosmogonic theories of the astronomers, has now given place to the 'conservation of energy' alone as the fundamental basis of existence. It is exceedingly difficult to picture this abstract energy out of which all things are formed, and the idealist philosophers have claimed, not without justification, that the scientists have, in fact, reduced all material to a spiritual basis, thus inadvertently overturning their own materialistic conception of the nature of the universe. There is, however, one form of energy that can be shown to exist independently of matter. This is 'electromagnetic radiation,' better known in its special form of 'light.' A light ray penetrating space is, in fact, pure energy, the stuff of which the universe is made: so dreamlike has the modern conception of reality become.

It is a strange fact that although the atomic structure of matter was deduced by philosophic thought as long ago as the time of the ancient

---

1   Alexander Philip of Brechin anticipated this conclusion from philosophy reasoning alone as long ago as 1885, as is elaborated in his dynamic *Foundations of Knowledge*, although the existence of radium and the cosmic disintegration of matter were undreamed of at that time, when the mechanistic conception of the nature of the universe was at its height.

Greeks, a similar atomic structure of energy was not advanced by philosophers. The discovery of the atomic nature of matter came as no surprise to philosophy, confirming as it did a long-standing metaphysical conception, but the recent discovery of a discontinuity in energy by experimental science has been entirely unexpected, as it was anticipated in no way by the classical theories. Why the mind should accept the infinite division of energy without scruple, while rejecting the infinite division of matter, is not very clear: but the fact remains that experimental science has demonstrated beyond all question the existence of a discontinuous structure of energy as of matter. There is, however, no standard 'atom' of energy: there are, on the contrary, 'quanta' or bundles of energy of an infinite variety of sizes, each quantum depending in size upon the frequency with which it 'acts.' These quanta are obviously unsatisfactory as universal units owing to this diversity, as we should naturally expect to find one common building block at the basis of existence, not an infinite variety. The Law of Relativity again comes to our assistance with a valuable analogy. Einstein has shown that space has no real existence independently of time, and substituted for three-dimensional 'space' the four-dimensional continuum of 'space-time.' Is it possible that we must not take energy itself as the basis of the universe, but consider a combination of energy and time? In fact, there is one fundamental constant that has within recent years appeared as the result of experiments in subatomic physics, which does combine energy and time. This is Planck's constant 'h,' which is the product of a quantum of energy and the period of time through which it acts. Large quanta follow very rapidly upon one another, each quantum operating through only a minute period of time, while small quanta are much less frequent, operating through much longer periods. In each case the product of energy and time is the same, which is a most significant fact, and it would seem clear that the fundamental basis of existence is to be found in these units of action or 'energy-time.' The longer the period over which one of these units of energy-time is distributed, the smaller will be the amount of energy available at any one instant. Just as the universe is extended through a 'space-time' continuum, so it is composed of an 'energy-time' substance.

When we accept the 'monist' conception of the universe as composed of one primitive substance, we must find some explanation of the apparent diversity of material objects and phenomena with which we are surrounded on all sides. The only effective solution would seem to be that the monist substance, whatever it is, must be composed of an untold number of particles or units, and the diversity of apparent forms is caused by the various combinations and arrangements of these primary units. All

Introduction

the soldiers of a regiment may be very similar in appearance, but a few minutes at any barrack square during drill will soon show the immense variety of formations into which they may be arranged. Actually the world of nature would seem to be formed from the primary units of energy-time by a series of integrations, to use a mathematical term, each 'integration' producing a new 'unit' formed by the combination of units of a lower order. In this way 'planes' of existence are denned, which have their own laws and conditions, and are sharply differentiated one from the other. Bodies on a higher plane of existence differ from those on a lower by the greater complexity of their organization. The whole scheme of nature seems to be devoted to the attainment of higher and higher degrees of organization, more and more complex combinations and permutations of energy-time substance.

The first integration transforms the 'monist' energy-time into the dualist condition of counter-strain, which we term positive and negative electric charge. How this is effected is at present unknown. Physicists know no natural means by which 'protons' and 'electrons,' the smallest units of positive and negative charge, can be produced from Planck's units of action, although modern astronomers assume the disintegration or mutual annihilation of protons and electrons to form quanta of radiation as the fundamental basis of their cosmogonic theories.[2] Protons and electrons do, however, clearly retain evidence of their energy-time origin, as their mutual revolution under the influence of electrical attraction shows the same strange discontinuity as we know in the case of radiation, the possible orbits of an electron about a proton being limited to certain definite dimensions, which are determined by the number of energy-time units involved. Furthermore, the latest investigations of the nature of protons and electrons has revealed that they can scarcely be regarded as material bodies, but rather as centres of energy subject to the same laws as radiation itself.[3]

The second integration is that it combines and arranges the electric charges of protons and electrons to form the 'atoms' of matter. These

---

2   As this disintegration is supposed to take place under the extreme conditions of heat and pressure in stellar interiors, the converse process of integration may well be held to occur under the converse conditions of extreme cold and diffusion which pertain in interstellar or inter-galactic space.

3   As Sir James Jeans has said in *The Mysterious Universe*, '. . . the tendency of modern physics is to resolve the whole material universe into waves and nothing but waves. These waves are of two kinds: bottled-up waves, which we call matter, and unbottled waves, which we call radiation or light.'

are apparently composed of a massive central nucleus around which revolve numbers of free electrons, and the positive and negative charges are so arranged that the nucleus is endowed with exactly sufficient positive charge to counterbalance the combined negative charges of the revolving planetary electrons. In this way a model solar system is produced where electric attraction takes the place of gravitation, but a strange difference is to be found in the fact that the planetary electrons do not attract one another like the planets in the solar system, but repel one another on account of their like charges. This enables several electrons to revolve at the same orbital distance from the nucleus without any possibility of collision. The more distant the orbit from the nucleus the greater the number of planetary electrons which can share it, as their interval being greater their mutual repulsion does not become disruptive. Successive rings of electrons surround nuclei of advancing mass, until a total of ninety-two is reached. These ninety-two possible combinations form the elementary atoms or 'monads' of terrestrial chemistry, out of which all other material bodies are formed. How these atoms are integrated from their constituent protons and electrons is still a mystery, as only the simplest atom of hydrogen can be produced naturally from the association of a single proton and a single electron.[4]

Disintegration, however, is well known in the case of the most complex 'radioactive' atoms when the nuclei spontaneously eject protons and electrons, and it is largely from the investigation of radioactivity that subatomic construction has been revealed.

The third integration occurs when atoms join together to form 'molecules.' It appears that atoms with a few electrons to spare after inner rings are completed wish to divest themselves of these supplementary electrons, while atoms with incomplete rings of electrons strive to complete their rings by 'borrowing' spare electrons from other atoms. These two kinds of atoms, known as 'metallic' and 'non-metallic' respectively, enter readily into combination with one another, satisfying their mutual desire for completed rings, and are held together by the electric attractions which ensue from the interchange of electrons. Obviously the complexity of molecular construction must depend upon the power of combination of the individual atoms. Those with half-completed rings requiring the

---

4   In this connection it is important to note that Dr. Millikin has shown the existence of exceeding powerful radiation from interstellar space which he believes to be caused by the integration of hydrogen atoms to form the more complex atomic systems.

greatest number of electrons to complete them, or conversely having the greatest number of electrons to spare after the completion of an inner ring, will have the greatest power of combination, and we shall expect to find such atoms as the basis of the more complex molecules. Actually carbon with only half its secondary ring of electrons forms the extremely complicated molecules associated with organic life, while silicon, which has only half its tertiary ring, is at the basis of most of the compound substances that form the rocks of the earth's crust. As there are ninety-two atomic monads, the possible variety of compounds is very large, obscuring all trace of the original monism of existence. Indeed, a great science of chemistry has been built up to investigate their formation and interaction. On this plane of existence, contrary to the conditions on the lower subatomic plane, integration is not only possible by natural means, but forms under the name of 'Synthetic Chemistry,' an established branch of the science. Even 'organic' carbon molecules of great complexity have been built up from their elements, atom by atom.

The fourth integration is the most critical of all, as it attains the ultimate limit of inorganic development and opens up a new vista of still more complex organic integration. As atoms can combine to form molecules, so molecules in their turn can be arranged in ordered formation to produce 'crystals'. Unlike chemical combination, however, crystallization does not introduce any further extension of variety, for as a general rule only identical molecules of the same substance will combine to form crystals. On the other hand, molecular integrations are still more easily affected than atomic combinations, as a mere change in the physical conditions under which a substance is dissolved in a liquid may cause it to come down in a precipitated mass of crystals. Here is none of the inherent stability of atomic and subatomic existence but a delicate state of reaction to external conditions of temperature and pressure. The ordered arrangement of nature is at last revealed to the naked eye in the mathematical structure and delicate symmetry of crystalline forms. The inorganic series reaches its ultimate height of complexity in the molecular integrations of quartz and basalt, granite and diamond.

While for the vast majority of chemical substances crystallization forms the limit of organization, it is merely the stepping-stone to the higher integrations of the organic series. In order, however, to attain the power of further development a crystalline substance must be formed which possesses the ability to maintain itself under a considerable variety of conditions. It must escape from the automatic dependence upon temperature and pressure, which is the characteristic of cruder crystals, and adapt itself to its surroundings. This ability of adaptation and interaction with external conditions is gradually developed by the more complex crystalline substances, especially those formed by the compounds of carbon, until certain 'fluid crystals' are produced which possess a certain power of motion as an additional aid to adaptation. Of these fluid crystals the excessively complex chemical compound 'protoplasm' possesses the powers of motion and adaptation to the high degree that we term 'life.' Protoplasm is essentially crystalline, in that it can only develop its adaptative power of 'life' in the presence of water, just as sugar and salt only produce their dynamic powers of crystallization and solution when immersed in liquid. The similar appearance of the precipitation of crystalline substances to the growth of organic structures, pure coincidence as it may be, is not without its significance.[5]

As protoplasm alone among crystalline substances possesses the attribute of 'life,' and has the ability of forming higher integrations of organization, the metaphysical system has returned in a sense to a new and higher 'monism' of living substance, from which all animate bodies are formed. The existence of this second 'monism' has encouraged philosophers to regard organic existence as something entirely distinct from inorganic, to assume a creation of living substance subsequent to and distinct from the original creation of inorganic material. Organic chemists, however, find that the chemistry of life differs only in its complexity from the chemistry of inorganic matter, and feel assured that protoplasm, despite its unique properties, is no more than an extremely complicated chemical substance. Just as all existence is built up of monist energy-time, so all living creatures are formed of 'monist' protoplasm. How protoplasm itself came to be formed remains a complete mystery, as all attempts to produce it in the laboratory have hitherto failed, but as it is the one substance capable of maintaining itself under a considerable variety of conditions once produced, and possesses, furthermore, the power of increment or growth, it would seem that some accidental chemical association in the azoic seas of early terrestrial history, however infrequent and improbable such an

5   Actually the interactions of protoplasm with its surroundings are undoubtedly not only physical but to a very large extent chemical as well, which is to say that it absorbs floating and dissolved materials other than protoplasmic matter, and adapts them to its own use, ejecting such waste products as it does not require. To simplify the development of the argument, however, this chemical attribute of protoplasm has been omitted above, as it has no direct bearing on the nature of protoplasmic matter, which is admittedly 'super-molecular.' Other 'inanimate' fluid crystals possess similar powers of 'eating' assimilable material, as has been shown by Otto Lehmann and others.

accidental association might be, could give rise to the whole of the present wealth of life on earth.

The fifth integration is only applicable to protoplasmic matter, as all other chemical substances show no power, at least under terrestrial conditions, of entering upon higher organization involving further integrations. Out of this one substance two forms of microscopic cell are produced very much on the analogy of the formation of protons and electrons from energy-time. Once more a monist substance integrates to form a dualism of opposing forms: indeed, the systematic integrations of organic existence reproduce in a second cycle the primary integrations of the inorganic world. On the one hand a jelly-like cell is produced capable of voluntary movement, and on the other a cell with hard, shell-like walls is formed which is highly resistant but incapable of bodily movement. This dualism of cell structure is of the highest importance, as it is reflected in the vital distinction between the animal and vegetable kingdoms throughout biology; animals being formed of jelly cells and plants of cells with rigid walls. How this differentiation of cell structure came about is as much a mystery as the origin of protoplasm itself, its solution lying in the dim and distant past of life upon earth far beyond the hope of our knowledge, unless laboratory experiment comes eventually to our assistance.[6] An important new development on this more complex plane of existence is the appearance for the first time of the inherent power of reproduction. Both animal and plant cells grow rapidly by the absorption of suitable materials, but there is a definite limit to the size to which a single cell can attain. When this limit is approached the cell splits into two, and each new cell enters upon an independent career as a reproduction of the original parent cell.

Following the analogy of the inorganic series we would expect the next stage in organic development from the dualism of animal and plant cells to be a further integration producing a limited number of monad forms equivalent to the atoms of chemistry. Actually, owing to the complexity of organic structure, a monadic differentiation of cell-forms is possible without any further integration. Both animal and plant cells can adopt a very considerable variety of sizes and shapes suitable for an equivalent variety of modes of life, and it is from these monadic forms that further organic development becomes possible. The organic series retains its essential parallelism with the inorganic,

---

6   Since the above was written, an American biologist claims to have produced living cells from 'raw material' taken from the brain of a calf after all cellular structure had been destroyed.

but produces its elementary monads by the differentiation of cell-forms instead of by an integration of primary units.

The sixth integration takes place when numbers of cells combine to form a multicellular organism. This combination is not in the nature of a mere colony of similar microorganisms, such as are frequently formed in the human body by parasitic bacteria; it is, on the contrary, a highly complex organization in which differentiated cell-forms undertake varied functions in the service of the whole community. It is, in fact, by means of the power of cellular differentiation, already described, that the multicellular organism can be produced, the various structures and organs of the higher organism being formed of cells best adapted to the several functions required of them. The production and reproduction of these multicellular organisms follows a peculiarly organic course in that, unlike the conditions of inorganic existence, the development of organic forms is not determined exclusively by external conditions, but a certain inherent vital urge impels the organism to an ever-advancing adaptation to its environment, and even to a modification of the environment in its own interest. Certain lower forms have attained an almost perfect adaptation to a certain definite mode of life, and have remained unchanged through untold ages: but organic life is ever seeking higher forms of development, new modes of life, more complex internal organization. Again and again in the past history of life upon earth new cellular differentiations in the service of the organism have produced new organs and new structures by means of which a great advance in the mode of life of the organism has been made possible. All these changes are excessively slow compared with the rapid reactions of chemical and crystalline existence, and form the basis of the gradual evolution of ever more complex forms of life, as revealed by past geological strata. Just as in the inorganic series, the combination of differentiated monadic cell-forms leads to the production of an almost unlimited variety of multicellular organisms, three-quarters of a million distinct species being recorded by modern zoologists. Indeed, zoology surpasses even chemistry in the immensity of its field. Reproduction on this plane is most mysterious, as all multicellular organisms reproduce themselves by means of one single cell ejected from the organism. This cell grows and splits into two, the two into four, the four into eight, and so on, just as do the lower bacteria: but in some highly obscure manner the single original cell contains in a concentrated form all the fundamental characteristics of the parent organism, so that the cellular community formed by the division and re-division of the original reproductive cell is controlled and developed to form by degrees an almost exact replica of its parent or parents. As reproduction by this means does not involve the destruction of the parent organism, 'Death' intervenes as a 'natural' means of removing less developed forms and making place for their more complex descendants.

A seventh integration would seem at least a theoretical possibility when we have already traced six successive stages of the formation of higher organizations by the combination of units of a lower order. The question suggests itself, whether multicellular organisms cannot themselves combine to form 'super-organisms' of a higher order, in which each constituent organism serves the communal whole. There would seem to be nothing impossible in this suggestion, even if we do exclude herds and packs of animals, among which no real differentiation of function occurs. In the insect world, at any rate, the communities of the ants, termites, and bees immediately suggest themselves as cases of 'super-organisms' in being, when each ant or bee serves the communal whole as subserviently as a body-cell serves the multicellular organism itself, and a very considerable amount of differentiation of function in the service of the community is developed. The fact that a beehive, for example, forms a new superorganic entity, distinct from the individual bees of which it is composed, is clearly revealed, when we seek the controlling mind that orders the complex workings of the hive as a whole. Obviously the 'queen,' burdened as she is with the whole communal duty of reproduction, is not the ruler of the hive. Indeed, we often find, as Maeterlinck has pointed out, that the 'queen' is actually coerced by her 'subjects,' when her actions would be detrimental to the interests of the hive. It would clearly be ridiculous to select any one single worker, much less a single drone, as the ruler, and we are hence compelled to assume some indefinite communal spirit shared by every member of the hive, which is the real arbiter of communal action. This superorganic hive 'spirit' it must be that directs the sudden general attack of the whole community against a threatening enemy, that determines the proper moment for 'swarming,' and generally regulates the communal action of the hive as a whole on all occasions when such concerted action is necessary. In the ancient insect world the seventh integration with the formation of superorganisms of a higher order has long since taken place, and the hives, ant-heaps, and termite-hills form new living entities as individual and distinct, as active and intelligent, as any higher animal.

Such, then, are the seven fundamental integrations of the monist energy-time substance of the universe, which may be arranged as follows:

Civilization As Divine Superman

ENERGY-TIME		**PROTOPLASM**
	MONISM	
Discontinuous structure		Power of adaption
First Integration		Fifth Integration
ELECTRICITY		**MICRO-ORGANISMS**
	DUALISM	
Protons (+) and electrons (-)		Animal and plant cells
Second Integration		(does not cover)
ELEMENTS		Differentation of cell forms
	MONADS	
92 different atoms		
Third Integration		Sixth Integration
COMPOUNDS		Multicellular Organisms
	PLURALISM	
Unlimited variety of molecules		Unlimited variety of species
Fourth Integration		Seventh Integration
CRYSTALINE STRUCTURE		**SUPER-ORGANISMS**
	ORDER	
Limit of inanimate organization		Limit of animate organization

Chapter I

The Real Superman

The great philosophic event of the nineteenth century was the discovery of the principle of evolution in biology by Darwin and Wallace. This discovery was an event of such immense importance, of such an epoch-making nature, that for a time human thought was unduly concentrated upon biology to the exclusion of other branches of philosophy, in which no such startling progress had been attained.

The publication of *On The Origin of Species* by Charles Darwin brought the obscure science of biology suddenly before the public in an arresting form, and following intense controversy the pioneers of evolution were successful in proving beyond all reasonable doubt the truth of their biological premises. The height of the struggle was marked by the famous duel between Huxley and Bishop Wilberforce at Oxford in 1860, after which the Darwinians were generally accepted as having made their point. This triumph of the evolutionist school in the development of biological science was a great advance, but unfortunately it has had unexpected reactions upon human thought in many branches of philosophy that have nothing to do with biology. Public attention had been concentrated upon the great biological controversy to such an extent, the public mind was so fascinated with the personal application of biological theories that it could only return to the contemplation of other problems of philosophy through the rose-tinted spectacles of Darwinism.

The word 'evolution' was on everybody's lips: the belief in a general amelioration of mankind and of all human institutions accepted as proved. Quite without reason biological premises were applied to all the sciences, as if Darwin had discovered some master-key to all human knowledge, rather than an underlying principle of biology alone. The reason of this general delusion is not far to seek. No other branch of philosophy had ever produced such an optimistic outlook as evolution offered in biology; in fact, philosophy had, in general, been inclined to stress the pessimistic view of the cosmos. When at last an optimistic principle came to light, the temptation to promote this isolated discovery to a general principle of philosophy became too strong for the control of reasoned scepticism. As the rapid progress of material invention and the unprecedented prosperity of the latter part of the nineteenth century seemed to confirm the optimistic evolutionary view of human affairs, by the beginning of the twentieth century 'evolution' was firmly established in human thought as the one underlying basis of the cosmic scheme. Indeed, this tyranny of biological premises over philosophy continues almost unabated to the present day, although from the European point of view, at any rate, the events of the last twenty years have shaken the unbounded optimism of the previous century.

Nietzsche is the great figure of the close of the nineteenth century. Completely under the influence of Darwinian theory, he attempted to transfer the principle of biological evolution to form the basis of a new ethical system of morality. He considered that the evolutionary advance of life on the biological plane inevitably presaged a similar advance of man as a civilized being to produce what he terms a 'superman': but he found that the conception of a higher human destiny on earth according to the premises of evolution required a new moral code of ethics. This new code of ethics was promulgated by Nietzsche, and is the essence of his philosophy. He showed that all existing systems of morality were antagonistic to the advance of individual man and to the evolution of the superman, especially was this the case with the 'slave-ethics' of Christianity. If the evolutionary creed had any value as a basis of human development, then the future of the race was paramount. Hence everything must be sacrificed to the production of the coming 'super-man.' Not only must the community bow the knee to the great newcomer, but the budding genius must realize his own great destiny and command a right of way for his upward progress. He must be relieved of the restrictions of humanity and consideration of others, and regulate his conduct only by the tenets of the new system of 'master-ethics' constructed for his especial benefit. The 'supermen,' these new moral giants, like H. G. Wells's unconscious caricatures, the children in *The Food of the Gods*, were destined to dominate the earth, and mere pygmies of ordinary men must give place to them at sight. Such was the new 'ethics' of that 'great blond beast,' the superman, super only in his overbearing selfishness. Undoubtedly Nietzsche, with his German logic and lack of humour, carried the evolutionary theory to the point of absurdity, unconsciously and painstakingly disproving his premises by a reductio *ad absurdum*, exposing the nakedness of the evolutionary creed as applied to human affairs once and for all. Certainly his edifice of 'master-ethics' upon which the superman was to rise to domination has failed to capture general approval, although inevitably attracting interested admiration as a magnificent feat of logical architecture, somewhat akin to the non-Euclidean geometry of Gauss in its non-Christian perversity.

The Real Superman

The ideal of the superman has been restored from this alpine height of absurdity to the more reasonable level of human attainment by no other than George Bernard Shaw, who, in his *Man and Superman* and *Back to Methuselah*, has given his utmost support to the very modern principle of 'eugenics.' Shaw's conception of the manner in which evolution is to change human nature has at least the merit that it is practical and well within the means of us all. While Nietzsche stressed Darwin's thesis of 'natural selection' in the struggle for existence, and conceived the future superman as surviving and flourishing beyond his fellows by dint of superior ability and brutal disregard for other less able competitors, Shaw, on the other hand, stressed Darwin's other thesis of 'sexual selection' applied by reasoning beings to the betterment of the race and the elimination of degenerates. While Nietzsche taught the 'survival of the fittest,' Shaw proposed the 'survival of the select,' which is a very fine and real distinction. Yet even Shaw, in his later development of the subject, has been tempted to emulate Nietzsche, and his 'Methuselahs' have a vague and shadowy resemblance to 'supermen,' although they are offered in a whimsical flight of fancy rather as a possible future reward for faithful eugenists than as a serious evolutionary suggestion. It is perhaps significant that despite all the vast prestige offered by Shaw's support, 'eugenics' remains a perfectly ludicrous subject. Mankind is, perhaps, too wise rather than too foolish when it refuses to take the question seriously. One is oppressed with the feeling that all the effort and goodwill expended by the evolution-haunted eugenists is somehow wasted, like a blow in the empty air aimed at a target that does not exist. Perhaps it is the unconscious realization of this futility that awakens the laughter of the sceptical.

In its invasion of modern thought the biological principle of evolution has entered even more strongly into the realm of history. Obviously the ardent evolutionist would attempt to make his dogma of upward progress apply not only to biology, to the advance of primitive man from the ape, but to world history since the advent of civilization. Despite repeated disappointments, he returns again and again to the attempt to marshal the facts in accordance with his preconceived theory, and as often he is repulsed by the hard reality of historical record. He cannot overlook the immense bulk of the Pyramids, yet they are relics from the grey dawn of civilization: he is confronted by the astounding legal code of Hammurabi of Babylon, four thousand years old: he contemplates the cultural glory of ancient Greece: then he turns to the destruction of the Roman Empire by barbarian Goths and Vandals, to the long-drawn horror of ignorance and barbarism during the Dark Ages that followed, before the first tentative efforts that led to the present civilized era. If he is wise he abandons the attempt. Yet after a period of complacent observation of the self-evident upward swing of modern civilization he becomes once more convinced that the world is progressing, and makes one more valiant effort to squeeze world history into the evolutionary mould. Such are the new 'World Histories.' In order to obscure the lack of uniform tendency in the historical period, prehistoric man, and even the whole biological series from the first poor amoeba in the primeval ocean to the ape, are brought in to redress the balance. H. G. Wells is the foremost of these evolutionary historians, who seek an underlying tendency of progress in history. His Outline of History is conceived to give material for his naturally optimistic view of the cosmic aim, as a sort of counterpoise to his literary pictures of the millennium to come. In order to gain a comparatively uniform appearance of progress he has been compelled not only to bring in the aforesaid amoeba, ape, and primitive man, but to minimize the very real triumphs of ancient peoples in comparison with those of recent times. On this account he has come into conflict with the classical scholars of Oxford and Cambridge, who consider not without justification that Greece and Rome have been dismissed too slightingly in his scheme of things.

It cannot be too strongly emphasized that history and biology are two distinct subjects, and that the discovery of evolution as the basic principle of the latter has no real bearing upon a discussion of the former. It would be just as reasonable to look a little farther back into the cosmic scheme, and expect to find some significant inspiration in astronomy. We would find a record of the gradual cooling of the earth from incandescence to the seat of life, but, if we were to attempt to predict on that account the gradual calming of human passions and the final lethargy of an apathetic generation upon a freezing earth, we would be dismissed as absurd. Yet the attempt to find an analogy for the development of civilized man in the animal kingdom is as ridiculous. History must be freed from this present tyranny of biological premises before an attempt can be made to understand the real inward meaning of historical development. When we cease to expect at all costs a comparatively uniform advance from one triumph to another in world history, then the true structure may reveal itself. As long as we regard history as a further exhibition of the evolutionary progress of biology, we only add quite unnecessarily to the natural historical perspective that makes recent history loom so much larger and more important than ancient. Only when we have learned to dissociate ourselves from the natural European point of view of world geography and from the natural modern outlook upon the past can we undertake to term ourselves 'World Historians.' In order to attain this essential objective standpoint it is absolutely imperative that we abandon any preconceived theory such as that of evolution which tends to exalt modern achievement upon a pedestal and degrade past attainments to a mere staircase of approach to the monumental level of modern civilization.

The failure of evolution to supply a satisfactory philosophic basis for world history is most readily explained by the suggestion that mankind has with the advent of civilization attained a higher plane of existence upon which the laws of the lower biological plane no longer hold good. Throughout the metaphysical series with each step of integration on to a higher plane primitive laws are superseded by more complicated ones. The following list of fundamental principles may be associated each with one of the several planes of existence.

ENERGY-TIME   LAWS OF RADIATION

First Integration

PROTONS AND ELECTRONS   LAWS OF ATTRACTION AND REPULSION

Second Integration

ELEMENTARY ATOMS   LAWS OF MOTION OF PLANETARY ELECTRONS

Third Integration

COMPOUND MOLECULES   LAWS OF CHEMICAL AFFINITY

Fourth Integration

CRYSTALINE STRUCTURE   LAWS OF MATHEMATICAL ARRANGEMENT

Fifth Integration

MICRO-ORGANISMS   LAWS OF REPRODUCTIVE MULTIPLICATION

Sixth Integration

MULTICELLULAR ORGANISMS   LAWS OF EVOLUTION

Seventh Integration

SUPERORGANISMS   NEW LAWS (?)

We should infer from the above that the failure of the evolutionary principles of biology to supply an explanation of the historical development of civilized man is to be accounted for by the assumption that in a state of civilization a new superbeing comes into existence, as real and distinct as the communal 'spirit' that directs the actions and reactions of the insect communities of hive and antheap, and that on the plane of existence of this superbeing entirely new laws come into effect.

Turning for comparison to the earlier critical integration from bacteria to multicellular organisms, it is, of course common knowledge that many cells go into the formation of every complex organic body. The human body, for example, is a conglomeration of numbers of various cells, which all obey one central direction largely located in the subconscious mind. Most of these cells are confined in a fixed position in the body, but some, like the blood-cells, are conveyed by the blood from one part to another, and the white corpuscles appear to have the power of penetrating the tissues at will. Yet all are under one strict discipline, and even the freely moving white corpuscles or phagocytes are absolutely under bodily control, acting, indeed, as the defence force of the body against invading microbes. Thus from the point of view of the amoeba or microbe the human body is a supercellular organization. From the point of view of nomadic tribesmen roaming the steppes beyond the bounds of civilization, like swarms of microbes, civilization must appear also as a superhuman, that is, superindividual, organization. The nomad observer sees a variety of human cells engaged in various tasks, which tend to maintain the communal welfare, and themselves forming the body of the civilized community. The solid flesh is comprised of many millions of peasants tied down by law or economic pressure to a fixed position on the land. The blood of trade and commerce carried by merchants and caravans passes in the pulsations of finance along the artery-like trade routes, which form an all-embracing network throughout the land. The great metropolis sits in the midst like a brooding brain, and controls the whole vast organism by the administrative service, which is the nervous system of civilization. Should the nomadic tribesmen attempt to break into the body of the community and spread like teeming microbes from a breach in the frontier defences, then for a time all normal functions of state are suspended, the body is filled with the fever heat of national resistance, and uniformly clothed soldiers move in ordered discipline along the arterial roads like white-clad phagocytes to meet the amorphous invader, repulse and destroy him. Indeed, if the struggle be prolonged, new soldiers will be recruited from the very bones of the state until victory is won, or civilization collapses under the strain. The attack of nomadic tribes is usually repulsed, the fever of national emergency subsides, and orderly life is resumed: but if civilization is old and enfeebled, death may result, especially when communistic cancer, that mutiny of the body cells, that refusal to carry out the allotted task, has undermined the constitution. As superindividual organizations, the human body and civilization have interesting points of resemblance.

Under this analogy the suggestion is confirmed that the abrupt break with evolutionary premises evident upon the dawn of civilization is an indication of the advent of a new superorganism, which is formed of many individual human beings, as is the human body of many individual cells. Although a large degree of free-will seems to be left to the individual, in point of fact upon the vast majority of civilized men a certain definite form of service to the community is enforced. Each is as inexorably bound down to his own particular task as any body cell. In fact, the boasted freedom of the individual in a civilized community is always more of an illusion than a reality, and even the leaders of the community are far more servants of the superorganism than heroic free agents moulding history.

Civilization itself is the superhuman force that expresses and realizes the ideal of the 'superman.' It is futile to seek a superman in personal individual human development at some distant future date, when the real superman, civilization is already engaged in building towering skyscrapers driving great tunnels, constructing huge liners and vast airships linking the lands with radio, and investing mankind with the collective attributes of supermen. We might just as well expect to find a 'super-microbe' as large as a horse, when it is obvious that the multicellular organism has long since superseded any such monstrosity. The Nietzschean 'Supermen' and the Shavian 'Methuselahs' are no less monstrous individual perversions in the superorganic world of civilizations in being. Civilization is not a biological process in the upward progress of mankind: it is a 'super-biological' force governed by 'super-biological' laws, directing the actions of mere men to the realization of its higher aims, the very realization of the 'superman.'

Before the end of the last century, Herbert Spencer had already traced the parallelism between civilized society and the human body, glimpsed earlier in this chapter, with a masterly insight. On the other hand, in his promulgation of the modern science of 'sociology' Spencer was as much under the influence of biological premises as his contemporaries. He conceived sociology purely as a continuation of biology, and was at much pains to trace a progressive upward tendency in society through the ages. Spencer was capable of recognizing in civilized society a superorganism in being, but he continued to apply the principles of biology to society in exactly the same manner as to species of animals. That this is justified when applied to amorphous unorganized primitive society may be true, but obviously individual evolution breaks down with the advent of civilization. Under the influence of the biological trend of thought in his time, Spencer failed to appreciate the full value of his epoch-making conception of civilization. He was also infected by the Manchester school of economic individualists, with their doctrine of laissez-faire, so that he marred the unity of his superorganism by an undue emphasis upon individual freedom, within the bounds of society, to which the twentieth century has already set so many limits never anticipated by the Victorian era.

Actually individual life has ceased to be even a remote possibility to civilized man, and as he lives through civilization, so he must of necessity live for civilization. He can no longer turn to and hunt for his food, or appropriate some cattle and tend them for their products, or even cultivate the ground and grow cereals. These tasks have become the specialized business of the few and high mysteries to the many. Hence as civilized man can on no account support himself outside the social organization of civilization, any more than a body-cell outside the human body, he is as absolutely dependent upon the well-being of the civilized community as is a body-cell upon the health of the human body, and owes a definite debt of service to the community, if only from the strictly materialistic argument of self-interest. That this is truly the case Spencer, inspired by the individualist sentiment of the nineteenth century, was ever at pains to deny, but modern observers appreciate more fully the power of society to impress its will by unwritten law and more emphatically by economic pressure upon the individual. Spencer, like every philosopher, was a product of his time, and was unable to realize the inward meaning of his original appreciation of the nature of the social organization, because he lived in a time of revolt against central government, and refused to admit that the individual could become the slave of the State to the extent of the body-cell or the more convincing parallel of bee or ant. His whole intellectual environment revolted against such a conception of tyrannical central government. In these days, on the other hand, when individualism is dying a lingering death, the idea becomes less revolting.

To America plutocratic control of society by means of the huge trusts has reduced the inalienable right of Americans to become millionaires from the ambition of every newsboy to a mere hollow mockery. In Italy and Southern Europe generally dictatorships have ordered the actions of the individual with astonishing attention to details. Soviet Russia applies economic pressure similar to that of the American trusts to restrict individual economic activity and bring all trade organization into the hands of the State-controlled syndicates and co-operative societies. The day of the individualist seems gone for ever. Even in Western Europe his freedom of action is more restricted from year to year, and conservative statesmen solemnly declare that 'the day when the individual might do what he liked with his own is past.' There is today no longer any strong public opinion opposed to the conception of the truth of society as a superorganism.

The appearance of the superorganism is claimed as an explanation of the sudden break with gradual individual evolution at the beginning of the historical period. It is not true that, as is suggested by the sociological theories of Spencer, society has gradually evolved through the hunter-nomad-agricultural stages of primitive life to the eventual organization of civilization. On the contrary, evolution would seem to have proceeded gradually and uniformly to the point of agriculture, and then of a sudden given rise to the new superorganism, 'civilization.' The fact of a sudden break with the past cannot be ignored. As agriculture produced a sufficiency of surplus material to supply giant nourishment, the superman sprang suddenly in full splendour from the fields of the patient peasantry. The agriculturists have tilled the soil and produced quite unconsciously the 'Food of the Gods' upon which a new race of supermen has been bred. Ever since have the puny peasants eyed askance and with much misgiving the product of their self-sacrifice, the giant civilizations that stride in magnificent steel-clad splendour about the earth. The 'superman' is come. He already orders the affairs of mankind. We are all His subjects, subservient to His will.

There is, however, a further important consideration which arises when the civilized community is regarded as an organism of a higher order, a factor that inevitably failed to appeal to Spencer with his tendency to merge biological and sociological development into one long, gradual process of advance. Natural organisms are not static; they pass through a regular series of changes, which constitute a life-course. From birth through childhood, youth, maturity, and old age the human organism shows at each period a typical form, and a practised observer can judge the age of all but the most exceptional individuals to within a very few years. No one expects a human being to remain unchanged for an unlimited period. There is an inevitable rise to maturity and decline to senility. Each individual attains a certain height of achievement, and then gives way to make place for the next comer. Yet Spencer has ignored the obvious conclusion that his superorganism is as susceptible to such a fundamental law as life and death, growth and decline, as any other natural organism. This rhythm of individual development is the absolute basis of organic life, and remains as unexplained and inexplicable as the nature of life itself. If the civilized community is an organism of a higher order, there is no reason to expect that it should escape this rhythm of life and death, growth and decline, that marks all other exhibitions of the 'life-force.'

The substantial divergence from Spencer's theory of the gradual passage from biological evolution to sociological evolution with no sharply defined line of cleavage, is that with the advent of civilization the slow evolutionary progress of primitive society is suddenly quickened into the rapid individual growth of the first superman civilization. The new superorganism is born and grows according to the natural laws of individual growth, and this giant growth suddenly catches up mankind to heights of attainment impossible to the slow processes of biological evolution. It is in the nature of a superorganism that it cannot be formed by the gradual advance of evolution. It was no process of gradually increasing bulk in an existing series of natural organisms, such as produced the elephant or the whale, that gave birth to civilization. On the contrary, such a new superorganism consisting of numberless individuals of a lower order can only come suddenly into existence when the will and the means of co-operation and specialization give rise to the organization of society, and the conception of the living reality of civilization. Such a process is obviously not gradual. Evolution may bring primitive society gradually up to the point when co-operation is both desirable and practicable, but when that point is reached no further slow process is required. The new functions of civilization will at once begin to operate, and the first social organism will embark upon its career as a higher order of existence. Civilization springs full grown from primitive society like Aphrodite from the sea-foam!

Certain bounds of attainment, however, restrict even the vast possibilities of a superorganism. It may reach a certain height of achievement, even an extraordinary peak of achievement, but it must inevitably decline and collapse, as must every other organism when it has passed its prime. This is the main consideration that Spencer entirely failed to grasp. He considered his social organism to be immortal and uniformly progressive, never a natural if higher organism susceptible to the laws of growth and decline common to other forms of life. Actually a superficial study of history shows that civilization is far from a uniform process, but is broken by dismal periods of barbarism into separate great epochs of culture. Each of these marks the life-course of a superman civilization which has dominated history for a time to decline and collapse into a blaze of primitive nomadic conquest, until a new superman civilization arises Phoenix like from the ashes of the old. Here is no uniform scheme of human endeavour, but a vast spectacle of the repeated cultural efforts of great organisms, rising and flourishing, striving against one another, conquering and destroying one another. The lack of uniformity in social progress, the apparent setbacks, the unexpected cultural triumphs of peoples at the dawn of history, are all capable of explanation in such a world of higher beings, the supermen of social organization, for whom men have lived and died, and through whom they have attained heights undreamed of by that true individualist, primitive man. The world is the field of vast forces, which direct and sway the puny leaders of men, who seem to control human destinies; great, unseen influences that emanate from the immense superorganisms that are the highest expression of the cosmic scheme. Civilization is not the servant of man. It is his master and tyrant; the superman that directs and enforces his actions to the greater glorification of Himself, and grants him the immense advantages of co-operation and specialization only as a reward for abandoning his freedom of action to the higher aims of the communal spirit.

CIVILIZATIONS
PAST AND PRESENT

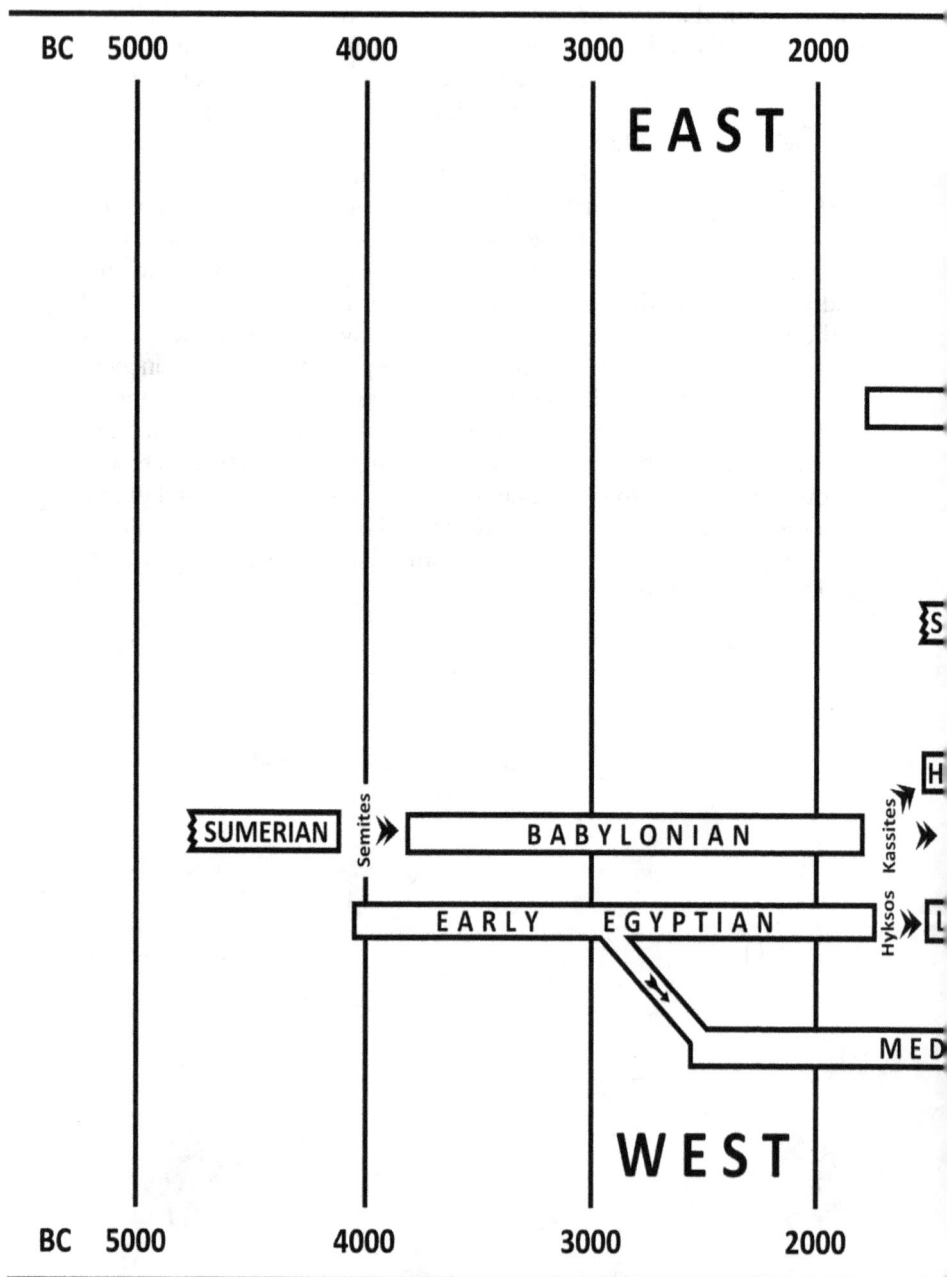

BC	5000	4000	3000	2000

EAST

| SUMERIAN | Semites ≫ | BABYLONIAN | Kassites ≫ | H |

EARLY   EGYPTIAN

Hyksos | L

MED

WEST

BC	5000	4000	3000	2000

S

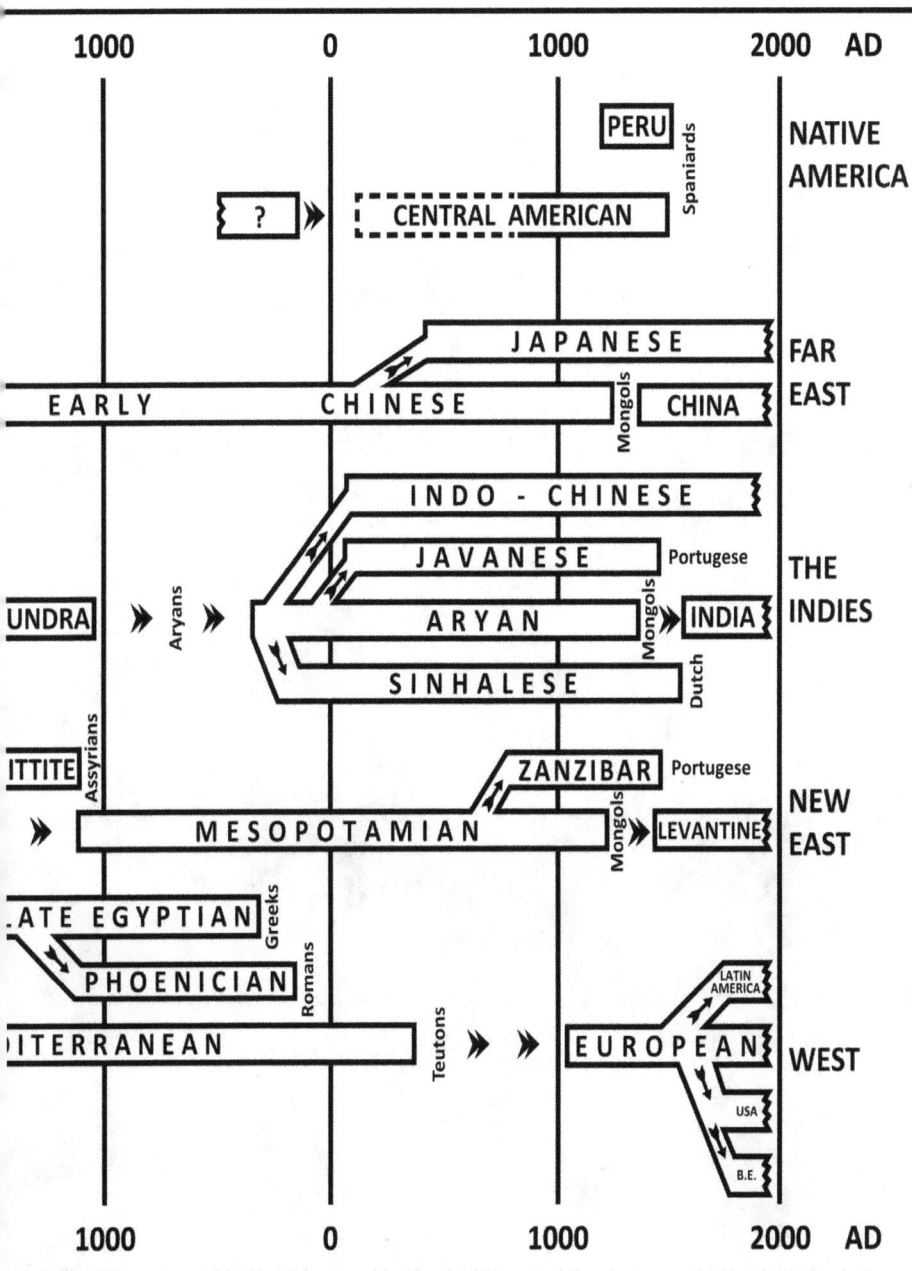

Chapter II

Civilizations: Past And Present

World history is not really concerned with primitive man and primitive society. World history is essentially the study of civilization, and civilization can only begin when mankind has passed through the preliminary stages of primitive society to a sedentary agricultural life. This distinction has been largely obscured by the desire of the evolutionary Darwinians to merge biology and history, and find a gradual evolution of civilization out of primitive society. The popular division of 'historical' and 'prehistorical' is much truer to fact. There can be no real history, for example, of the Red Indian tribes of the North American continent before the coming of the white man: none has ever been attempted. Nor can a history of equatorial Africa or the South Seas be reconstructed, as the whole subject lacks the essential social and political structure without which such records as exist are a jumble of unrelated insignificant facts and no historical narrative. Even the history of the nomadic peoples of the northern steppes has had no reality of its own, and they have only gained an occasional place in world history when, under the name of Goths, Huns, Vandals, or Mongols they have swept away, some overripe effete civilization in an orgy of destructive purification. On these occasions every attempt to trace the 'history' of these peoples even a few decades before their irruption into the light of civilization has proved a hopeless task. Primitive society even as it has existed up to recent times is amorphous, lacking all political structure, and its existence is a mere biological state of being without any historical significance in itself.

Although a discussion of primitive society is no part of the task of world history, yet an appreciation of the nature of primitive organization before the advent of the first civilization is essential in order to understand the conditions under which it came into existence. Primitive society forms the amorphous ever-changing yet changeless background out of which civilization has emerged, and into which it occasionally relapses. It is the waste of waters out of which the solid structure of civilization has arisen and which is ever washing at the foundations of the cultural edifice, until it brings down the whole weakened framework and washes for a time over its ruins.

The most primitive being that can still be called a man is undoubtedly the hunter. It was a very important stage in the progress of man from the ape, when he abandoned the arboreal vegetarian life of the monkey for the terrestrial carnivorous life of the caveman. The sudden appearance of primitive man in the biological scheme as a carnivorous animal was a revolutionary occurrence, as all other carnivores were descended from the distant and widely divergent 'creodont' stock. Indeed, this revolutionary change of habit was a significant prediction of the higher destiny of man, and it may well be assumed that man would never have reached the level of civilization except by way of the roundabout carnivorous stage.

A hunting community, however, is far from civilization, almost as far as the apes themselves. The number of families that can subsist upon the game resources of even many square miles of forest land is strictly limited. The hunter's paradise of North America before the advent of the 'white man' could only support a few hundred thousand Red Indians, where today as many millions of Europeans could easily find a home. More serious, however, than the sparse population is the impossibility of effective co-operation between hunting communities for any cultural effort. The hunting peoples must divide and subdivide down to the small multiple family group of the tribe in order to gain a livelihood from the chase. Under such conditions there can be no real combination in any sense of the word over more than a very limited area. This is the cause of the chaotic ethnological disorganization of the typical hunting peoples. Untold centuries of hunting life on the North American continent, with the resultant division of the hunting society into many isolated tribal federations in occupation of local hunting grounds, gave full rein to ethnological divergence, so that the few hundred thousand Red Indians supply the student of languages with more entirely diverse tongues and allied dialects than the whole civilized world put together.[7] The hunter is still so dependent on nature, so little removed from the conditions of animal life, that all suggestion of civilization is obviously futile, and no buried city will ever be found in the typical hunter's paradise of North America.

The really vital upward step from complete dependence upon the caprice of nature came when primitive man began to order the lives of the larger ungulates upon which he depended for food. The primitive hunter cannot grasp the possibility that game is not inexhaustible, and regards periods of scarcity simply as 'acts of god.' The Red Indians and Eskimos, for example, were ever far too prone to indulge

---

7   The same is true of the hunting communities of the negroes in tropical Africa, where almost every village has its own dialect and every river valley its own language.

in prodigious slaughter and feasting, whenever game was plentiful, without the slightest conception that they were thus contributing to the very famine of which they went in fear. In the forest lands it was perhaps only natural that the primitive hunter should never appreciate the limited number of his prey. On the open steppes of Northern Europe and Asia, on the other hand, hunters following on the skirts of herds of cattle and sheep, horses and camels, could grasp the true state of affairs, and see with their own eyes that restraint in time of plenty was essential to avoid scarcity in time of famine. They would soon learn to drive off carnivorous animals poaching on their preserves, to be considerate of doe and young, restricting their killings largely to the male animals, and, in fact, gradually to develop a real concern for the well-being of their prey.

It was inevitable that the unceasing attendance of such hunter-herdsmen would in the end have its effect upon the gregarious nature of the herd. Even goats will inspire sheep with a feeling of leadership, which they will follow blindly, so that the continued presence of men would in the end overcome the natural distrust of the herd, and appeal as a form of guardianship and guidance to the gregarious mentality. At last the changing hunters would be accepted as benevolent leaders by the herd, and permitted to enter into the true vocation of herdsmen. When friendly relations are once established between primitive man and the herd, tremendous possibilities are opened. Cattle supply milk: sheep are shorn for wool: horses are used for traction and eventually for riding: camels are employed as beasts of burden. Primitive man has finally emerged from the hunting stage, and as a herdsman is no longer so dependent upon nature, is gaining a more definite control over his own destiny.

Politically speaking, the herdsman is known as a 'nomad,' as it is his custom to be ever on the move, seeking new pastures for his flocks and herds. Nomadic tribes are, however, still, despite their considerable evolutionary advance, incapable of real civilization, and lack independent history. There is the same sparseness of population, although, through the benevolent care of the animals of the herd, an equal area of country can support a far larger number of herdsmen than hunters. Nomadic tribes are limited to the size of the herds which can find pasturage in one locality, and any very large concentration of men in one place for any length of time is rendered impossible by the lack of pasturage for the huge herds required to support them. Furthermore, nomads require to be continually on the move to find new pasturage, should the original grazing lands become exhausted or burnt up in times of drought. Real co-operation in an attempt at cultural organization is thus as impossible as in the case of the hunting peoples, and the tribal unit, with its flocks and herds, is the limit of social organization, except when tribal federations are formed for the purpose of migration and the conquest of new pasturage further afield. This power of mobility is, indeed, the greatest advantage of the nomadic state of society, as the herdsmen can move with flocks and herds, women and children, at almost incredible rapidity over thousands of miles of country, in sharp contrast to the almost complete immobility of the hunter. Although as incapable as the hunting tribe of maintaining a fighting force at a distance, the nomad tribe can in time of war throw the whole tribal weight into motion and dash it against another nomad enemy or the bulwarks of civilization. Indeed, this very mobility and the continual conflict for the best pasturage, intensified by occasional drought, is the primary cause of the failure of nomadic life as a basis of real civilization. The nomads are condemned to form the outer sea that rages in restless tribal motion beyond the breakwater of civilization's boundary, and bursts through now and again to submerge some world-weary culture in a beneficial flood of primitive simplicity.

Before the advent of civilization, the world was the seat of these two, hunter and nomad, forms of primitive society. Their distribution was largely determined by climatic conditions. The American continent, however, presented a striking exception, in that there was, strange to say, in that land of prairie and pampas, no evolution of nomadic herdsmen from the normal Red Indian hunters.[8] In the Old World, however, both hunter and nomad tribes existed, each in its own exclusive area. Climatically and topographically the Old World is divided into a northern and southern section by a vast belt of desert that stretches almost unbroken from the Atlantic to the Pacific. This desert land consists successively of the Sahara, Arabian Desert, Persian Desert, the Pamirs, Tarim Basin, Gobi Desert. In Europe and Asia, north of this desert belt, nomadic society was predominant in the prehistoric period, and nomad tribes with flocks and herds wandered on the Russian and Siberian steppes, even penetrating into the park lands of Central and Western Europe. South of the desert belt in equatorial Africa, India, China and Malaya, on the other hand, hunting tribes held the forests, and even in the bush lands of Australia failed to develop any form of herdsman society. In Africa, however,

---

8   This may be explained by the fact that the teeming bison herds on the American prairies were both too formidable for domestication and too numerous for any need of conservation. It is interesting to note how soon the Indian hunters annihilated them when equipped with the white man's rifle.

south of the equatorial forests in the mixed deserts and park lands of the south and east, the negroes evolved nomadic habits and herdsman organization in apparent independence of the northern nomads. It is true that African nomadism never attained the height of the advanced northern form; for example, domestication was confined to cattle and never extended to horses, yet it is remarkable that the negroes should have been capable of this advance denied to the American hunters.[9] Thus at the dawn of history, at least in the northern part of the Old World, nomad and hunting peoples were no longer in direct contact with one another, being separated by the desert land, and while nomadism had made a complete sweep of the hunting communities north of the desert belt, it had failed to penetrate southwards beyond the deserts into the typical tropical-forest land. Primitive society had reached a state of stable equilibrium, practically dictated by climatic conditions, and the domains of nomad and hunter were sharply defined.

Agriculture is an obvious further stage in the upward progress of primitive society, yet a difficult one. Man had deliberately turned carnivorous in his descent from the trees to undertake the struggle for existence on the ground; as a hunter he developed all the dog or wolf-like tendencies of gregarious carnivorous life; even as a nomad herdsman he was still directly dependent upon animals for food. To revert to the vegetarianism of the ape was a complex mental process. It is true that the herdsman was indirectly vitally preoccupied with the question of pasturage for his herds, and soon learned to gather and dry fodder in summer for use in the scarcity of winter. On the whole, however, one is inclined to the conclusion that the hunting communities rather than the nomads gave rise to the first agriculture, while nomadism remained a sterile branch of the evolutionary stem. The hunter had not evolved so far from the original vegetarian ape, and was always addicted to eking out the uncertain diet of the chase with fruit and wild cereals. The further step to cultivation would not be too difficult, especially in regions where game was scarce and soil fertile.[10]

The advent of agriculture is of vital importance in the upward progress of man, because cultivation makes possible that co-operation and organization which is essential to the development of civilization. Those barriers to combination of cultural effort, already

---

9   There is just a possibility that the northern nomads penetrated through Arabia and Somaliland down the east coast of Africa, but this remains an improbable suggestion, considering the forbidding nature of the obstacles to such a migration.

10   Indeed, even the typical hunting tribes of the North American continent engaged in primitive cultivation to a certain limited extent.

pointed out in hunting and nomadic life, are entirely removed in an agricultural community. In such a state of society the whole people must be supported from one harvest to another on some form of preserved food, and dried cereals, tubers, etc., supply this need. This conservation of food in a compact vegetable form readily available and requiring no upkeep is an immense advantage over the conservation of live stock, which, although readily available as food, requires constant attention and upkeep. The agricultural community could maintain a large body at a distance for any length of time by supplying them with a sufficiency of preserved cereals, and they could concentrate any number of people upon one point and maintain them there without difficulty in the presence of a comparatively small storehouse of conserved grain.

These advantages over primitive society would not, however, be sufficient to attain civilization were it not that the efficiency of even primitive agricultural labour is such that a small part of the community is in a position to supply the rest with ample foodstuff. The remainder, being relieved of animal preoccupation with questions of food supply, are able to engage in the first tentative efforts towards cultural advance. With the production by the first agricultural community of food available in the compact easily transportable form of grain, and of a large surplus of such food, civilization becomes a possibility. The critical moment, the birth of World History, is reached. At once a difficulty of definition arises. What is this 'civilization' that comes of a sudden to transform primitive society into the living texture of World History? 'Civilization' is a much misused word, and can be made to mean many things in different mouths, so that it is necessary to make a special definition of the exact meaning it is intended to convey in this discussion.

Civilization is the attribute of a community, which, after meeting the absolute needs of its members, accumulates a surplus of production, and co-operates on a large scale to apply this surplus to the realization of wider, higher aims than the mere gratification of immediate individual wants.

In primitive society the accumulation of surplus production is scarcely possible to a hunting tribe, and is largely confined to excess live stock in the case of nomadic life, but it is in the vital matter of co-operation that primitive society is unable to reach the plane of civilization. Hunting and nomad tribes are in the very nature of their dependence upon animal life debarred from real inter-co-operation, and remain inevitably independent social units in the amorphous sea of primitive society. Agricultural life, on the other hand, can form the basis of civilization, because it produces an ample supply of excess food, and this food reserve enables co-operation on a large scale to be undertaken by a large section of the whole community in the service of higher cultural aims. Thus early agriculture gave rise almost immediately and spontaneously to early civilization.

It is a remarkable fact that all the earliest civilizations sprang up in that desert belt we have already described as separating the homelands of the nomadic and hunting tribes. At first sight this would seem to run directly counter to the supposition that civilization springs from agriculture, as these desert wastes would seem to be the most unlikely regions on earth for the first primitive efforts of the early agriculturists. Actually agricultural life began as a barely tolerated rival form of primitive society, and was driven to take refuge in the only regions unsuitable for its enemies. It can be readily understood that primitive society was bitterly hostile to agriculture, with its attendant dawning civilization. Hunters, who might welcome the beginnings of cultivation as a subsidiary source of food, would fiercely resist the wholesale clearance of forest land for cultivation on a large scale, as an impious interference with the sacred hunting grounds. Similarly the fencing-in of pasture land for cultivation would evoke the violent hostility of nomad herdsmen as a restriction of the traditional freedom of pasturage and a check upon free migration. Under these circumstances it is not surprising that the early agriculturists were compelled to make their first efforts at wholesale cultivation in the desert lands, where both the other forms of primitive society were at a disadvantage, and they found an opportunity to develop their arts undisturbed by either bloodthirsty hunters or land-jealous nomads.

Of course the actual waterless deserts of the Western Sahara, Eastern Arabia, Southern Persia, and Northern Mongolia could never become centres of agriculture, but here and there the desert belt was crossed by mighty rivers, which have all become the sacred rivers of early civilization. Nile, Euphrates and Tigris, Indus, Yellow River, they have all this in common, that they run during a large part of their course through sandy wastes. Prior to the advent of the first agricultural communities they must have presented a desolate enough appearance, indeed the Euphrates and Tigris have been allowed to relapse very much into that prehistoric condition. Sandhills probably stretched down to the limits of flood water, and dismal mud flats completed the landscape as far as the river banks. Although the mud banks left by such a desert river are extraordinarily fertile, there is not enough time between the annual floods for natural-sown vegetation to take seed and flourish, hence unless artificially cultivated and sown the annually flooded riverside areas remain desolate except for isolated palms and wind-sown fast-growing grasses. The first agricultural communities, however, taking refuge on the banks of these rivers from the severe struggle for existence in the tropical forests,[11] found that even under their primitive arts of cultivation, the mud flats proved amazingly fertile, and they were able to turn from hunting (or fishing) to purely agricultural life on the strength of the proceeds of their labour.

Thereupon they flourished and rapidly took possession of the entire river valley or valleys within the desert belt, accessible to their original settlements. Their revolutionary zeal was rewarded beyond all expectation. What may have seemed a miserable compromise with tribal hostility, a cowardly flight from human enmity to the endurance of desert hardship, proved to be the inspiration of civilization. A very few thousand years ago the few poor agriculturists scratching a living on the sandy banks of the Nile, Euphrates, and Yellow River must have seemed rather miserable creatures compared with the wealthy nomadic peoples of the northern plains, with their teeming flocks and herds, or even with the hunters of the tropical forests, at whose doors game was plentiful for the catching without the sweat of prolonged labour in the blazing desert sun. Yet those poor hardworking communities, the first real labourers the world had known, held the germ of future greatness, denied to the more flourishing nomads and hunters.

The multiple origin of civilization cannot be rationally denied, although certain misguided enthusiasts have sought to trace connecting links between the most ancient civilizations in different regions of the globe. An attempt has even been made to connect the culture of the widely isolated

American native civilizations with Asiatic inspiration: but the general similarity of forms common to all civilizations which is put forward as an indication of a single origin of culture has its real cause in the common brain structure of man, not in mutual inspiration. The important and deciding argument is that at least the early Levantine, Chinese, and American civilized communities were absolutely and profoundly ignorant of any other cultural system in the world beyond their own. On the banks of their desert rivers these first civilized peoples struggled to maintain their dearly won civilization in face of the hostility of fierce hunter and nomad tribes, quite oblivious of other distant peoples of strange colour and race engaged in exactly the

---

11   Or, in the case of the Euphrates and Tigris, fishers driven up the rivers from salt water.

same conflict in some other remote quarter of the globe. In fact, early civilizations much nearer to one another than the widely sundered examples given above have sprung into existence from primitive sources without any sign of mutual influence or even knowledge of the existence of the one by the other. For example, Egyptian and Mesopotamian civilizations were for many centuries ignorant of one another, and it was only late in their history that these cultural stocks began to effect mutual influence. Similarly at the time of the Spanish invasion, Mexico and Peru were only vaguely aware of each other's existence, and there is every reason for assuming that civilization sprang up independently in Central and Southern America. When it is fully realized that culture springs spontaneously from an agricultural community, the multiple origin of civilization need cause no particular astonishment, as it merely indicates the presence of a foregoing state of agriculture in the various original cultural centres, and as the attainment of the agricultural stage of primitive society is a natural and inevitable culmination of the evolutionary progress of primitive man it is quite possible and indeed probable that this final accomplishment would be reached independently by widely isolated primitive communities.

Six original civilizations, all of which have long since passed away, are sketched out on the next page:

ORIGINAL CIVILIZATIONS

SUMERIAN CIVILIZATION[12]

PRIOR TO 4000 B.C.

We know very little indeed of the earliest civilization on the plains of Mesopotamia. We are only aware that prior to the invasion of the Semitic peoples, and the rise of the Empire of Akkad, an aboriginal civilization of an advanced and complex nature existed, which was apparently destroyed by the barbarian Semites. This civilization was of non-Semitic Sumerian origin.

---

12   This was the prior civilization, the recollection of which gave rise to the famous Babylonian 'flood' myth. The 'flood' was not physical, but a metaphorical flood of barbarism, such as overwhelmed the Roman Empire.

EARLY EGYPTIAN CIVILIZATION
4000 TO 1800 B.C.

The early agricultural communities in the Nile Valley were united into one great empire by Menes of the I dynasty, who, coming from the upper Nile, founded Memphis at the apex of the Delta. He was followed by a series of autocratic Pharaohs, who built the many pyramids of Egypt to their own honour and glory. These eventually gave place to a period of local autonomy, when many cities up and down the Nile enjoyed independence under their own local princes, until they were finally reunited under the sway of the princes of Thebes on the upper river. These new Theban Pharaohs differed greatly from their Memphian predecessors in their benevolent care of the interests of their subjects, building great reservoirs and developing the irrigation system of the Nile, instead of erecting useless monuments. Gradual degeneration, however, followed, until Egypt was overwhelmed by an invasion of nomadic 'shepherds,' the Hyksos, from Syria, and the whole valley suffered devastation with fire and sword.

SUDRA CIVILIZATION
PRIOR TO 1000 B.C.

The earliest civilization in India is shrouded in complete mystery, and there are indeed many who question the existence of a native civilization in India prior to the invasion of the Aryans from Central Asia in the first millennium. The Vedic legends of the Aryans, however, record the existence of great stockaded cities side by side with primitive nomadic customs of life. These contradictory statements can only be assimilated by the assumption of a foregoing native civilization, that declined and was overwhelmed by an irruption of nomads from Central Asia through the passes of Afghanistan. It is, furthermore, highly significant that in the Hindu caste system the lowest caste of the Sudra, which is known to include the aboriginal stock, is that of the handworkers generally, who were graded far below the primitive Aryan peasantry, which is what we would expect to find when a nomadic people conquers a civilized one. Indeed, the appearance of Aryan nomads (traced ethnologically from the Central Asian steppes) beyond the desert belt in tropical India, in a habitat entirely unsuited to their nomadic habits of life, is difficult to explain otherwise than as the result of the attraction of the loot of a disintegrating native civilization.

Early Chinese Civilization
1800 B.C. TO 1250 A.D.

The Chinese agricultural communities on the Yellow River, like those on the Nile, were united by the cultural efforts of a series of autocratic emperors, who instituted a highly bureaucratic system of 'mandarin' government. In due course, however, this original autocracy declined, and the Chinese Empire split up for a time into a number of 'Contending States,' which engaged in intermittent civil war, until one local ruler conquered the others and reunited China. In the time of the Contending States Chinese civilization progressed exceedingly, producing the classical age of Confucius and spreading to the entire valley of the Yangtzi. Reunited under the prosperous rule of the Han dynasties, Chinese authority then spread deep into Central Asia, until Chinese armies actually reached the Caspian Sea, and Chinese caravans carried Far Eastern wares to be sold on the distant Roman markets. After several centuries of supremacy this vast empire fell, however, into a gradual and irregular decline, which weakened the traditional resistance to the unceasing pressure of the barbarian nomads from the north, until at last the original cultural region of the Yellow River and then the Yangtzi basin, fell into the hands of barbarian Tatars and Mongols.

Early Central American Civilization
PROBABLY PRIOR TO A.D.

The exceedingly complex political organization of the native civilization found in Central America by the Spaniards upon their invasion, and the existence of a fully developed 'flood' myth, recalling a previous period of civilization, comparable to the classical myth of Babylonia, very strongly suggest a former era of civilization prior to that known to history. The destruction wrought by the fanatical Spanish 'crusaders' was, however, so great that it is impossible as yet to confirm this supposition, and it will probably require many decades of patient archaeological research before the early history of this isolated region emerges from the mists of the past. The discovery of a well established chronological system does, however, give hope of eventual success.

Peruvian Civilization
1200? TO 1500 A.D.

On the other hand, the extreme simplicity of political structure shown by the great empire of the Incas in Peru would seem to confirm the native tradition of the comparatively recent foundation of this system. It is quite credible that Peruvian civilization dates from only a few centuries before the invasion of the Spaniards, and that the legend of Manco Capec, the first Inca and founder of South American civilization, is based on fact.

These six original civilizations have long since succumbed. The first generation of supermen has passed from the earth. Yet civilization persists today as vigorously as ever. There must be some manner in which the superorganism perpetuates the cultural impulse. According to the analogy of organic life, the most obvious manner in which this can come to pass is by the reproduction of the original civilization in an offshoot equivalent to the offspring of a natural organism. This can actually be shown to take place, although this is not the only manner in which culture is handed down from one generation to another.

In order to understand how this takes place it is necessary to appreciate the real spiritual nature of civilization, and its superman identity, independent of the nations and races through which it finds expression. Unfortunately, the historians of modern Europe are so strongly imbued with the nationalism which is the outstanding feature of our civilization at the present time, that they are far too much inclined to connect cultural effects with the races and nations which have been inspired by them. Thus they speak of Greek culture, Roman culture, even Gothic culture, as if civilization were an expression of the national or racial individuality instead of a higher superorganic quality quite independent of racial attributes. A superman civilization is not directly concerned with the nature of the individuals of which it is composed, and will pass with great readiness from a conquered race to its conquerors, or vice versa. Frequently in world history a form of culture has been passed on with almost perfect continuity from one people to another, as when Mediterranean civilization passed from the Myceneans to the Greeks, and later from the Greeks to the Romans. Civilization is a spiritual force, which is not confined to one particular race or nation, but may pass from race to race and from nation to nation.

It is in this manner that the inspiration of new offshoot civilizations occurs. Where no sharp geographical boundaries, such as high mountain ranges, vast expanses of desert, and in the case of continental civilizations the sea, restrict expansion, an original civilization may incorporate more and more territory and many primitive peoples before it is checked by contact with another rival superorganism. Such was the case with Early Chinese civilization, whose expansion to the present wide area of Chinese Empire was of such a phenomenal nature. Certain physical boundaries exist in the case of every civilization, and some, like that of Egypt, have been confined within very narrow limits indeed. Where such restriction of available area exists, the original civilization is definitely limited in expansion, as political and cultural unity can only be maintained within the prescribed area. The civilizing impulse, however, is such that it cannot be confined by mere physical obstacles, and spreads irresistibly beyond the most insuperable barriers in the course of time. When this takes place in the case of a circumscribed civilization, the cultural impulse, which has passed beyond the bounds of cultural unity, forms the focus of a new offshoot civilization, as it cannot be brought within the political sphere of influence of the original culture.

In the case of a true offshoot civilization, the cultural impulse, which carries the inspiration of civilization from one world region to another, is not accompanied by any large number of colonists from the homeland, who would for a time at least bring the two civilizations into one political unity. The native peoples in the further world region themselves adopt culture due to the inspiration of contact with the original civilized community. A certain amount of immigration is no doubt necessary in order to convey the full reality of culture, but this immigration is restricted to the amount that can readily be absorbed by the native race without altering its native character. Under these circumstances the offshoot civilization adopts the early primitive form of superorganic development and passes through all the typical phases of the superorganic life career. In fact, there is true direct reproduction of kind by kind as in the case of a natural organism. The original superman civilization produces a distinct replica, which possesses a life-identity of its own, and following its conception by inspiration passes through all the usual processes of growth and decline, outliving the original parent culture by many centuries.

OFFSHOOT CIVILIZATIONS

EGYPTIAN INSPIRATION

Early Egyptian civilization was the most restricted in area in the whole record of World History. It was confined by the surrounding deserts to the Nile Valley, and at no time did the early Pharaohs succeed in penetrating into Syria. It is therefore not unexpected to find that Egypt was the first source of offshoot civilization. Primitive maritime peoples of the northern shores of the Mediterranean and the islands of the Ægean came into contact with the advanced civilization of the Egyptians at the mouths of the Nile, and gradually became inspired to emulate the cultural achievements of the rich southern land.

MEDITERRANEAN CIVILIZATION
2500 B.C. TO 400 A.D.

Secure from the inroads of northern barbarians on the islands of the Ægean, a new civilization came into being and took the primitive form of an autocratic empire centred upon the palace of the Minoan kings at Knossus on Crete, the largest island. This empire flourished for many centuries before it eventually disrupted into a number of independent Mycenean states among the islands and upon the neighbouring mainland. An invasion of northern barbarians followed shortly, to overwhelm the mainland cities, but in accordance with the laws of superorganic development these incoming Hellenic peoples themselves adopted the civilization of the conquered Myceneans and carried it with an outburst of primitive energy to a much higher level. Indeed, such was the force of their cultural activity that, after withstanding the full assault of the ancient Mesopotamian cultural stock led by the all-conquering Persians, the Greeks conquered both Egypt and Mesopotamia, submerging both ancient civilizations in a flood of Hellenization, from which Egypt was never to emerge as a distinct cultural entity. After conquering the East, Mediterranean civilization turned to the West, and, crushing the Semitic culture of the Carthaginians, spread under Roman leadership to Spain, Gaul, Britain, and part of Germany. Materialism and degeneration now, however, overtook the ageing superorganism, and within a few centuries the vast Roman Empire had fallen to become the booty of a new inroad of northern barbarians, the Teutonic peoples pouring into the civilized lands of the south.

40

INDIAN INSPIRATION

India, like Egypt, although much larger, is as definitely restricted in area by the surrounding mountain ranges and the sea. There could be no question of an indefinite expansion of Indian civilization as a cultural entity, and hence when Aryan culture on the Indus and Ganges expanded under the inspiration of Buddhism to cover the whole peninsula, it was inevitable that offshoot superorganisms should be inspired in neighbouring regions overseas or beyond the mountain barriers.

JAVANESE CIVILIZATION
100 TO 1500 A.D.

The passage of the inspiration of Indian civilization to the Malay archipelago must remain obscure. We can only assume that it followed the trade routes with the rich East Indian islands. In the absence of reliable historical records, we are unable to reconstruct Javanese civilization in detail, but enough is known from native chronicles and existing temples and antiquities to establish an amazing parallelism with the course of Aryan civilization in India. We find the same sequence of Buddhism, Brahmanism, and Islam, with clear indication that Javanese civilization always lagged several centuries behind Indian, for Islam only reached the Malay archipelago in the fifteenth century, shortly before European conquest brought native independence to an end.

INDO-CHINESE CIVILIZATION
100 A.D. TO PRESENT TIME

It is highly significant in the conception of civilization as a super-organic spirit distinct from the individuals of which it is composed that, although the Indo-Chinese peoples are drawn from the Chinese racial stock, they should have adopted Indian cultural forms, and preserve practically no trace of Chinese influence in their cultural development. There can be no question that civilization came to Indo-China, as it came to Java, through the zeal of Buddhist missionary enterprise, which followed the trade routes across the Bay of Bengal to the mouths of the Irrawaddy. The Burmese, as the most westerly of the Indo-Chinese peoples, were the first to gain cultural inspiration from India; and for many centuries a great autocracy ruled at Pagan until destroyed by a Mongol invasion from the north at the time of the downfall of Early Chinese civilization. Meanwhile culture had spread to Siam and Cambodia on the Pacific shores of the Peninsula, and a period of intense nationalist rivalry ensued between a number of independent states until checked by the arrival of European influence. Siam, however, retains to this day the tradition of independent Indo-Chinese culture.

CHINESE INSPIRATION

Although Chinese civilization was enabled to spread westward through Central Asia to an immense area, the actual fertile land suitable for agricultural development was limited by the mountains and deserts that encircle China proper, and it was only to be expected that Chinese civilization has also given rise to a cultural offshoot. By way of Korea the inspiration of the glorious civilization of China in the classical epoch passed to the islands of Japan, beyond the political control of the continental Chinese Empire.

JAPANESE CIVILIZATION
400 A.D. TO THE PRESENT TIME

Civilization was established in the Japanese islands by the absolute autocratic rule of the early Mikados, who organized a bureaucratic government on the model of the Chinese 'mandarin' system. Eventually the principal official of this bureaucracy, the 'Shogun,' usurped supreme authority, and the Mikados were restricted purely to their spiritual office as Shinto divinities. The power of the Shoguns was, however, soon disputed by the provinces, and the Japanese Empire split up into a number of warring principalities. This condition of disruption persisted for several centuries, until by the efforts of a trio of great statesmen Japan was once more reunited in the early sixteenth century. An effort was then made to invade China by way of Korea, which failed upon Japan losing the command of the seas, and the newly restored Japanese Empire retired into complete isolation from the rest of the world, as a protest against the aggression of the crusading Spaniards and Portuguese. This self-imposed isolation was only broken less than a century ago by American enterprise, but Japan has since advanced to the forefront of modern development in successful rivalry with the Western peoples.

Although original civilizations do produce offshoot civilizations in neighbouring world regions, as we have seen, this is not a sufficient explanation of the continuity of cultural descent. Propagation by offshoots merely extends the area of cultural development beyond the limits that can be covered by the original civilization without sacrificing its essential unity. The problem of the continuity of cultural descent in the original world region remains to be explained. It has already been shown that the four original civilizations of the Old World all eventually succumbed to nomad invasion, and yet the regions occupied by these civilizations have remained centres of culture down to the present day, if allowance be made for the later absorption of Egypt into the Mediterranean system. A further explanation of cultural descent from generation to generation of supermen is vitally necessary.

When a civilization collapses to nomad attack, the submergence in the flood of barbarism is never such that some remnant of the original community does not survive and continue to engage in agriculture. Large tracts may revert to nomadism, and their cultivated lands to pasturage for flocks and herds, but world history gives no example of the complete degradation of a civilized agricultural community to nomadic life, although sometimes, as in the destruction of Mesopotamian civilization by the Mongols, the remnant of cultivation has been a wretched fragment of the former wide expanse of civilized territory. If an agricultural community of any kind survives, it is obvious that, in accordance with the law of the spontaneous development of civilization from agriculture, eventually a new superorganism will emerge from the chaos of the 'Dark Age.' Furthermore, however destructive the barbarian regime may have been, some record of former magnificence, some monuments of the past, must survive the loot and rapine of the nomad hordes, so that the natural rebirth of civilization is accelerated by the inspiration of the earlier triumphs of cultural co-operation. Just as an offshoot civilization is inspired across a physical obstacle by the existence of an original civilization in a neighbouring world region, so a descendent civilization is inspired across a period of barbarism by the former existence of a parent superorganism.

It is clear that, as the primary cause of the rebirth of civilization is the re-establishment of those primitive conditions which gave birth to the original superorganism, the life-course of the descendent will be strictly parallel with that of the parent civilization. The factor of inspiration, too, is in every case very strong, and there will be much greater family resemblance between civilizations in the descendent series than between offshoot and original civilizations in different world regions. This is very clearly shown in the tyrannical ascendancy of Mediterranean cultural forms over the 'renaissance' art of European civilization, which is paralleled by similar tendencies to reproduce the glories of a former 'classical age' in later civilizations throughout the world, perhaps most strongly in China and Egypt.

The several cultural stocks may be traced in successive descent from their original ancestral civilizations as follows:

DESCENDENT CIVILIZATIONS

MESOPOTAMIAN STOCK

PRIOR TO 4000 B.C.

SUMERIAN CIVILIZATION

Original destroyed by the invasion of Semitic barbarians.

BABYLONIAN CIVILIZATION[13]

3800 TO 1800 B.C.

It was under Sargon of Akkad, one of the Semitic leaders, that civilization revived once more on the Mesopotamian plains. He conquered a large empire from the Persian Gulf to the Mediterranean, and founded a dynasty which maintained this realm for some centuries. Gradually, however, the power of Akkad declined, until a general political disruption enabled the cities of the plains to recover their independence. The city of Ur rose for a time to a position of prominence, but only to be eclipsed by the semi-barbaric Elamites from the hills of Persia. It was Hammurabi of Babylon who expelled these foreigners, and built up the benevolent system of government perpetuated by his famous Code of Laws. Babylon became a flourishing metropolis with a population of millions in a prosperous empire, but degeneration inevitably followed, and Babylonia relapsed by degrees into a chaotic barbarism; after the invasion of the Kassites, a further irruption of Semitic peoples.

---

13 An unsatisfactory term, but one hallowed by much usage in this sense. Actually Babylon did not rise to prominence until the last stage of this cultural system.

MESOPOTAMIAN CIVILIZATION
1100 B.C. TO 1250 A.D.

Mesopotamian culture emerged from the Kassite barbarism and the temporary predominance of Egypt under the leadership of the autocratic kings of Assyria, who extended their empire by degrees over the whole of the plains, and even penetrated through Syria to conquer the entire valley of the Nile up to the famous city of Thebes. Exhausted by the military enterprise of the Assyrian kings, this great empire fell when at its very height before the onslaught of the Aryan Persians from Central Asia. In strict accordance with the superorganic conception of civilization, however, we find that these barbarian invaders adopted the existing Assyrian autocratic form of government, restoring Mesopotamian ascendancy over Egypt and extending the new Persian Empire to the borders of India and through Asia Minor to the shores of the Ægean. Here they came into contact with the youthful civilization of the Mediterranean, and a titanic inter-cultural contest ensued, from which the Greeks under Alexander eventually emerged victorious, conquering the Mesopotamian Empire to the borders of India itself. The Greeks, as an oligarchic caste of conquerors, formed a definite further stage in the development of Mesopotamian culture, but were superseded in the course of time by the restoration of Persian (or Parthian) independence. Finally, Mahomet and the early Caliphs from Arabia swept away the Graeco-Persian oligarchy to make place for the new benevolent system of brotherly equality before Allah, which is the essence of Islam, and the Caliphate spread its vast domain from Spain to Central Asia. This great empire, with its capital at Bagdad, fell, however, comparatively soon into a state of plutocratic degeneration, until completely destroyed by the repeated invasions of Turks and Mongols.

LEVANTINE CIVILIZATION[14]
1450 A.D. TO THE PRESENT TIME

The invading Turks settled in Asia Minor, and, simi-civilized by contact with Islamic culture, alone possessed the necessary virility to restore civilization, despite the violent hostility of the Mongol barbarians in possession of the traditional cultural homeland of the Mesopotamian plains. Driven to the west by the terrible Timur, they finally conquered the remnant of the Roman Empire at Constantinople, and established a

---

14   A term adopted in its widest sense to indicate the displacement of Mesopotamian culture to the West.

great autocratic Sultanate in its place. This new Turkish Empire rapidly subdued Eastern Europe until the Turkish armies stood before the walls of Vienna. The Black Sea and Eastern Mediterranean became Turkish lakes, and Mesopotamian culture entered upon a new lease of life. The inevitable decline and disruption of this autocratic empire has reached its ultimate conclusion within living memory, and the new virile nationalism of the Near East indicates the advent of a further stage in the life-career of modern Levantine civilization. Indeed, there is certain evidence that this extreme nationalism has not been without its effect upon the smaller nations of Southern and South-Eastern Europe.

EGYPTIAN STOCK

EARLY EGYPTIAN CIVILIZATION
4000 TO 1800 B.C.

Original destroyed by the invasion of the Hyksos shepherds.

LATE EGYPTIAN CIVILIZATION
1500 TO 300 B.C.

The princes of Thebes furthest distant from the Hyksos invaders from Syria first raised the standard of revolt against the shepherds, drove them from Egypt, and followed them into Syria. They established a new powerful autocratic government at Thebes, and led their armies through Syria to the Euphrates, temporarily subjecting Mesopotamia to Egyptian authority. Conflict between Pharaoh and High Priest of Ammon, however, weakened this great empire, until it eventually broke up into a number of autonomous states, which fell victims to the successive invasions of Ethiopians and Assyrians from south and north respectively. During the temporary eclipse of Mesopotamian power, while Assyria fell to the Persians, Egypt recovered her independence for the last time under several dynasties of benevolent Pharaohs, who rivalled the early Theban Pharaohs in their works of public benefit. This was, however, no more than a short respite before final submergence in the turmoil of the first great struggle between Mesopotamian and Mediterranean culture, and Alexander, welcomed as the liberator of Egypt, did no more than substitute the foreign rule of the Greeks for that of the Persians. Henceforth Egyptian civilization became merged with the Mediterranean cultural stock, and ceased to have any independent existence of its own.

MEDITERRANEAN STOCK

MEDITERRANEAN CIVILIZATION
2500 B.C. TO 400 A.D.

Egyptian Offshoot destroyed by the invasion of Teutonic Barbarians.

EUROPEAN CIVILIZATION
1000 A.D. TO THE PRESENT TIME

Civilization was restored to Europe by the efforts of the Catholic Church under the leadership of the Papacy after the failure of the grandiloquent 'Western Empire' of Charlemagne. The Church formed a powerful instrument of government, and for several centuries Rome (and Avignon) was the capital city of a united Christendom, while the unceasing conflict with Mesopotamia entered into a new phase with the organization of the Crusades by the Papacy.

After several centuries of hierarchic government, the provinces chafed against the centralization of Rome, and at the Reformation a typical national disruption produced the European states of recent memory, which thereupon entered upon a fierce internecine struggle for the hegemony of the continent. After France and Germany have both been frustrated in their endeavours to attain this supremacy, the advance of democratic sentiment in Northern Europe tends to the formation of an international United States of Europe, while Southern and South-Eastern Europe fall more and more under the influence of reviving Levantine culture.

INDIAN STOCK

SUDRA CIVILIZATION
PRIOR TO 1000 B.C.

Original destroyed by the invasion of Aryan barbarians.

ARYAN CIVILIZATION
300 B.C. TO 1400 A.D.

47

Civilization was restored to India by the Aryan leader, Chandraguptau, working partially under Greek influence, owing to the inspiration of the presence of Greek colonies founded by Alexander in the Punjab. The Gupta dynasty organized a powerful autocracy in the Ganges Valley, and adopted under Asoka the magnificent Buddhist religion. Buddhist missionaries rapidly extended the sway of Aryan culture over the entire Indian peninsula, and even carried the inspiration of Buddhism overseas, as we have seen. On the Indian mainland the ascendancy of Buddhism was to be shortlived, however, and with the passing of the autocratic empires of the north the Brahmanic faith of the original Aryan invaders was restored.

India became for centuries disrupted into a large number of independent 'raja' principalities, and continuous internecine warfare raged up and down the peninsula. No single state ever gained the ascendancy over the whole of India before the period of Hindu rule came to an end with the invasion of the Moslems from the neighbouring cultural system of Mesopotamia. Despite the success of the Moslem conquerors, India never became wholly converted to Islam, and the Moslem community remained in the minority except in the Punjab until the Mongol invasion of Timur from Afganistan put an end to this cultural epoch.

INDIAN CIVILIZATION
1550 A.D. TO THE PRESENT TIME

Although India did not suffer as did Mesopotamia from the Mongol invasion, a period of chaotic disorder followed the fall of the Moslem Empire at Delhi, until the Mongols themselves under Akbar restored cultural unity by means of a powerful autocratic regime. This Mogul Empire covered the greater part of the peninsula, but lasted a bare two hundred years before its power passed to provincial governors or Nabobs and to independent Mahratta princes. These latter formed a confederacy with the object of controlling all India, but were finally conquered by the British, who had formed a trading fraternity on the Indian coasts. Since this time the British have ruled in India as a foreign caste of conquerors, but there are ample signs today that this supremacy cannot be much longer maintained.

CHINESE STOCK

EARLY CHINESE CIVILIZATION
1800 B.C. TO 1250 A.D. ORIGINAL

Destroyed by the invasion of Mongol barbarians.

LATE CHINESE CIVILIZATION
1350 A.D. TO THE PRESENT TIME

It was in Southern China that a native revolt arose against Mongol rule, and within a few years the barbarian leaders had been expelled once more into their desert fastnesses. The Ming dynasty then set about the restoration of Chinese civilization, organizing a powerful centralized autocracy on the traditional 'mandarin' lines. Comparatively soon, however, disruptive tendencies became apparent, and the provinces rose against Pekin. The Manchu Tatars thereupon took advantage of the embarrassment of the Government to conquer the whole of China, and set themselves up as a foreign oligarchic caste superior to the native Chinese. This Manchu regime lasted some three hundred years, until shaken and humiliated by the advent of European influence. A native revolt based on Canton then restored Chinese independence, but only to inaugurate an unstable revolutionary regime, which has by no means assumed a permanent form today.

CENTRAL AMERICAN STOCK

EARLY CENTRAL AMERICAN CIVILIZATION
PROBABLY PRIOR TO A.D.

Original Cause of destruction unknown.

LATE CENTRAL AMERICAN CIVILIZATION
100? TO 1500 A.D.

The advent of a new civilization in Central America after the decline of a former cultural era is indicated by the legend of the pyramid builders of Cholula, which is a striking parallel to the legend of the tower of Babel in Babylonia. It appears that the Toltecs formerly held autocratic sway from ocean to ocean, but at the time of the Spanish invasion this empire had long since been disrupted to form the many Mayan city-states, which were threatened by the aggression of the semi-civilized Aztec peoples from the north. The even less civilized Spaniards, however, swept both Mayan and Aztec culture away in a common destruction. There is one case of a short-lived civilization, which it is difficult to group as either an offshoot or descendant culture.

DESCENDANT-OFFSHOOT CIVILIZATION

HITTITE CIVILIZATION
1500 TO 1100 B.C.

After the decline of Babylon, a long period of disorder followed on the Mesopotamian plains before the rise of Assyria. This period is partially filled by the Hittite culture of Eastern Asia Minor, which arose as a form of descendant offshoot of Mesopotamian stock. Subbiluliuma laid the foundations of a powerful autocratic empire, which dealt with Egypt and Babylon on equal terms, and his descendants held Northern Syria for several centuries, until the rise of Assyria drove them back into the mountains of Asia Minor, where traces of their culture lingered on into Greek times.

A third manner in which civilizations are propagated is similar to that of the production of 'offshoot' cultural systems, but in this case civilization is conveyed directly to the distant world region by colonization instead of indirectly by inspiration. We may say in this case that the colonial civilization has 'budded off' from the parent stem. It is in the nature of things that this form of propagation, like that by offshoots, should mainly proceed by transportation overseas, and it is since the conquest of the seas by European mariners in the sixteenth century that this form of cultural reproduction has come into its own. The opening up of ocean communications has made it possible for European civilization to send colonists to distant parts of the globe in numbers sufficient to prevent any absorption of the colonizing community by the native peoples. The colonies are at first retained under the political control of the homeland, and the influence of home culture is fully maintained over them. Thus at first sight it appears that through efficient marine transport the original civilization has found means of unlimited expansion overseas. Actually this apparent power of unlimited expansion is illusionary.

The fact is that despite the easy communication by sea with the homeland, and the initial coincidence of colonial and home culture, there is a very strong tendency to the divergence of colonial from home civilization, which deepens as time passes.

The colonial community is after all situated in an entirely different world region from that occupied by the home people, and is subjected to entirely different conditions of life. It is not surprising that the culture exhibited by the colonists should develop at a different rate from that of the homeland. At first this has no more serious effect than a gradual growth of misunderstanding and a different point of view of world affairs; but friction may in time rise to the breaking-point, and the already divergent colonial community will break away from home control and give rise to an independent superorganic civilization. Thus the propagation of culture by colonization takes the form of a budding off of the colonial culture from the main home stock, and its eventual complete separation by social cleavage.

In this manner the colonial civilization does not revert to primitive forms, as in the case of an offshoot, but continues the life-course of the original civilization in a divergent form from the status it had attained at the time of the budding off of the colonial community.

The following divergent civilizations have been formed by various forms of cleavage from the parent stem:

Divergent Civilizations Egyptian Origin

Egypt, limited as it was by the surrounding deserts, was the origin of the first divergent, as of the first offshoot, civilization. Following the ejection of the Hyksos, the powerful autocratic Pharaohs of the New Empire at Thebes invaded Syria and extended their sway as far as the Euphrates. The peoples of Palestine and Phoenicia, already semi-civilized by contact with Babylonia, became organized as part of the Egyptian cultural system under the bureaucratic government of the New Empire, and many records of local tribute and submission to, authority are to be found in the Egyptian archives of the time. Later, the power of Thebes declined, undermined by the hostility of the priesthood of Ammon, and the local princes of Palestine and Phoenicia revolted against Egypt.

PHOENICIAN CIVILIZATION
1100 B.C. TO 50 A.D.

Separated by the desert wastes of Gaza from their former rulers, the peoples of Palestine and Phoenicia attained for a time complete cultural independence, during which period the magnificent literature of the Hebrew Bible was written. Later, the advance of Assyria from the north swept Israel into exile, and threatened Judah with a like fate. Meantime, however, the Phoenician cities of the coast lands were turning their attention to the seas, and their maritime enterprise laid the foundations of colonial settlements far into the Western Mediterranean. Even the all-conquering Assyrians and Persians found it wise to patronize this wealthy merchant people, and they survived in considerable prosperity until finally overwhelmed by the Greeks, their jealous maritime rivals. Yet even after the famous Tyre and Sidon had fallen before Alexander, Phoenician power found another focus in the west about the great colonial city of Carthage on the coast of Northern Africa. Here for another couple of centuries the maritime enterprise of Phoenicia found full scope, before the rise of Rome brought Carthage to destruction after the epic struggle of Hannibal against fate. At last Jerusalem alone remained in precarious enjoyment of a partial independence, and the last hopes of Phoenician culture centred about the small Jewish community of the Palestinian uplands. Despite a great religious revival, however, led by the fanatical Maccabees, the Jews were compelled to give way before the gradual rise of Roman power, until the final catastrophe of the siege and destruction of Jerusalem brought the ultimate doom of a great cultural system. Yet such has been the amazing resistance of Phoenician culture that there are plenty of traces of Semitic influence to be found in modern European civilization, which, erroneously referred to 'Jewish' origins alone, are obviously still incompletely assimilated relics of the glorious Phoenician past.

INDIAN ORIGIN

India, like Egypt restricted in area, has also been the origin of both offshoot and divergent civilizations. Following the adoption of Buddhism by Asoka, Aryan conquest spread rapidly through the Deccan to the southernmost point of the peninsula. Not content with this success, the Aryans crossed over to neighbouring Ceylon and soon conquered the whole island. Makunda, one of the sons of Asoka, then became king of this outlying province of the vast Indian Empire, and established a powerful Buddhist hierarchy in the island.

Sinhalese Civilization
200 TO 1600 A.D.

When the rest of India disrupted into numberless Raja principalities and returned to the primitive polytheistic Brahmanic faith of the Aryan peoples, Ceylon remained true to Buddhism and to its original Asokan dynasty. The hierarchy remained in autocratic control of the island, repelling several Indian invasions and definitely establishing the cultural independence of Ceylon. Only after many centuries did an eventual political disruption give rise to the era of the 'Seven Kingdoms,' which finally succumbed one by one before the aggression of Portuguese and Dutch. Even today under British rule Ceylon retains many highly distinctive cultural traits differing widely from those on the Indian mainland, clear indications of an independent cultural destiny.

MESOPOTAMIAN ORIGIN

The ancient cultural stock of the Mesopotamian plains has given rise to surprisingly few either offshoot or divergent civilizations. Taking the short-lived Hittite culture as the only example of the former, we have only one example of the latter. When the Caliphate was at the height of its prosperity, merchants from rich Bagdad, emerging from the Persian Gulf on the way to India, found that the trade-winds tended to carry them down the coast to the rich shores of tropical East Africa. There they founded colonies on what was later to be known as the Zanzibar coast.

Zanzibar Civilization
800 TO 1500 A.D.

Refugees fleeing from the tyranny of the Caliphate found sanctuary in the Zanzibar cities in such numbers that they invested these centres with a strong spirit of cultural independence of the homeland. Furthermore, the spirit of Islamic democracy favoured a rapid intermixture with the natives, until the prosperous Zanzibar communities were strongly marked with negroid characteristics. Upon the collapse of the Caliphate before the onslaught of the Mongols in the thirteenth century, Zanzibar survived in continued prosperity despite the cessation of trade with Mesopotamia, exchanging the products of Africa with those of the opposite shores of the Malabar coast in Western India. It was this trade that the Portuguese brought to a sudden end in the sixteenth century, finally and irretrievably ruining the vast cities of Zanzibar, famous for their many mosques through the whole of the Orient. Today little, indeed, remains to recall the magnificence of the past.

EUROPEAN ORIGIN

European civilization has been the most prolific source of divergent cultural systems known to history. This has been mainly on account of the conquest of the seas by European seamen, which opened up the oceans of the world as highways to all parts of the globe. Three distinct cultural systems have already diverged from the European stock, and it is highly probable that further developments will increase this number.

CREOLE CIVILIZATION
1500 A.D. TO THE PRESENT TIME

It was a significant coincidence that the discovery of America by Columbus happened in the same year as the fall of Granada, the last stronghold of the Moslems in Spain. Crusading armies, which had at last attained their goal of the expulsion of Islam from Spain, were released to extend their conquests to the New World overseas. Their fanatic zeal brought ruin and destruction to the Stone Age civilizations of Central America and Peru, and all the coasts of South America were rapidly colonized from the Iberian peninsula. At first the autocratic sway of the Spanish Crown, aided by the influence of the Church and Papacy, united Latin America in strict political unity with the homeland, but the dawn of the nineteenth century brought political disruption and the formation of the many local republics which still exist in complete independence to the present day. The divergence of Creole culture from European is revealed in many striking social and political differences.

AMERICAN CIVILIZATION
1650 A.D. TO THE PRESENT TIME

After Spain had conquered and colonized the rich civilized lands of tropical America, the bleak, inhospitable shores of North America alone remained for the settlement of the Protestant peoples of Northern Europe. Here England proved most successful, largely on account of the dogged determination of the democratic refugees, who found sanctuary in 'New England' after the collapse of the Commonwealth. It was when the home Government attempted to regain their control over these recalcitrant former subjects that revolution followed and America became independent. Since then the development of American civilization has followed the democratic tradition of the English Revolution, and the United States have formed the most highly developed democratic system in the modern world. The divergence in social and political forms from the still oligarchic Europe is very marked indeed.

Oceanic Civilization
1800 A.D. TO THE PRESENT TIME

Since the loss of the American colonies, and the final attainment of the command of the seas following the Napoleonic Wars, Great Britain has been enabled to enter upon a form of cultural divergence from the rest of Europe, organizing a vast colonial Empire overseas. The British have rapidly developed distinct differences from the peoples of the rest of Europe on account of the privileges and responsibilities of their colonial possessions, and there are many signs that further divergence may yet produce several further independent cultural systems from the far-flung British Empire.

Chapter 3

The Political Cycle

1. THE AUTOCRATIC PHASE

It is clear that civilization arises spontaneously from a state of agriculture. To begin with, an agricultural community is a typical barbarian tribe in which every man is engaged in cultivation, as every man in a hunting tribe is a huntsman and every man in a nomad tribe is a herdsman. There is at first no specialization of function which is the fundamental principle of civilization. Gradually, however, the agrarian tribe finds itself by dint of long-continued labour in the possession of a large excess of foodstuffs, or alternatively it finds that a small part of the community is capable of producing sufficient foodstuff to support the rest. As excess food is pure waste, the tribe naturally embraces the second alternative, restricts its output, and is faced with two problems. On the one hand, the greater part of the tribe is 'unemployed,' and on the other, a large amount of 'capital' in the form of excess grain is available for use. Now, unlike modern England, the tribe does not accept these strange facts as an affliction of the Lord upon decadent agriculture, but combines these two conditions of excess labour and excess food to embark upon an immense cultural enterprise. It does not allow its 'unemployed' to wander about the countryside in idle subsistence on a dole of grain from the labouring cultivators, but engages them in a variety of specialized undertakings in the service of the new dawning civilization. Armies are enlisted for defence, and, may it be whispered, offence as well: roads are built to open up the country: great irrigation works are constructed to increase still further the efficiency of agriculture. Indeed, 'leisure' from the direct cultivation of the soil is not allowed to become a tribal source of degeneration, but is exploited as an opportunity of organizing co-operation and achieving civilization.

The primitive tribe soon realizes the impossibility of dealing as individual tribesmen with the vast problems of the application of excess population and excess capital to the realization of civilization, and wisely delegates this task to a central authority, which gathers the talent of the community about it in the service of the cultural impulse. Autocratic government assumes of necessity the first place in the development of civilization. The amorphous prehistoric state

57

of barbarism must be concentrated into a definite coherent unity before culture can be attained, and it is only under the centralized authority of an autocrat that civilization can be given a cultural reality. The super-organism is brought to life and given a living form by the concentration of the economic and social powers of the community upon one centre. What little cultural ability may exist broadcast in the community is sufficient to establish civilization only when gathered in one focus.

Great things are possible to the first organized community under the guidance of autocracy denied to prehistorical anarchy. The debt owed by 'original' civilizations to the first despotic rulers finds recognition in the legends of several such cultures. Egyptian legend tells of the great Menes, who united upper and lower Egypt and founded the civilization of the Nile Valley. Native Chinese history is prefaced by a wealth of legendary material, which gradually and almost imperceptibly merges into real historical record. Several dynasties of great imperial autocrats are described as teaching the people the arts and crafts of civilization. In Peru the first of the Incas is represented as appearing in the country from across the water and civilizing a former barbarian people. Several 'offshoot' civilizations have similar legends.

The Greeks still retained legends at a late period of the great Minos of Crete, who ruled in autocratic splendour in a palace which was so large that it formed a 'labyrinth,' and extorted tribute from all the shores of the Ægean to his capital city of Knossus on Crete.

The Japanese still revere the earliest legendary Mikados, who ruled in Japan with absolute despotic power shortly after the conquest of the islands and the introduction of Chinese culture.

While the origins of 'original' civilizations are shrouded in legend, and must of necessity remain so shrouded, as it is only with the advent of civilization itself that recorded history begins, the restoration of civilization after an inter-cultural period of barbarism is a matter of historical record, and may be made the subject of direct study. In every case the first necessity of the restoration of the cultural impulse in a descendant civilization is a link with the preceding civilization through the dark age of barbarism to maintain the continuity of cultural descent. Here the biblical myth, drawn from Babylonian sources, of 'Noah' and his 'Ark' finds practical application as a symbolic illustration of the rescue of some of the cultural achievement of an 'Antedeluvian' (Sumerian) civilization through the 'flood' of

(Semitic) barbarian invasion to inspire the cultural revival of the later Babylonians. There have been many 'Noahs,' or rather 'Arks,' in history (as no one lifetime has ever sufficed to bridge the age of anarchy). Indeed, there is no record of any civilization in history being so entirely overwhelmed by nomad invasion, that some remnant of its culture has not survived to inspire a later age. In some isolated region or in some privileged community the continuity of the cultural impulse is maintained until the barbarian 'flood' subsides, and the 'Ark' of culture comes to rest upon a peak of autocratic authority spreading then by degrees the advantages of civilization to the noble highlands and the democratic plains.

The following 'Arks' may be discerned by the world historian afloat on the seas of barbarism:

- Thebes, under her petty princelets, struggling to maintain her independence of the Hyksos shepherd-kings of lower Egypt.

- Assur, on the upper Tigris, gradually freeing herself of the sway of the Kassite barbarians ruling in Babylon.

- Southern China, spared by Kublai Khan the terrors of Mongol loot and rapine, awaiting impatiently the day of revolt and freedom from the barbarian yoke.

- Delhi, burnt and devastated by Timur, crouching in her ashes until awakened to new life by the Moguls, Baber and Akbar.

- Angora maintaining Moslem independence under the Ottoman Turks, despite stunning defeat at the hands of Timur, until the capture of Constantinople laid the foundations of a new empire.

- Catholic Rome retaining the spiritual aura about the dead bones of the Roman Empire through the raids of Goth and Vandal, Lombard and Frank, to inspire the cultural achievements of modern Europe.

Although the struggle to maintain the cultural 'Ark' afloat and seaworthy, despite the storms of nomad migrations, may be severe, and the flood of anarchy may be of so long duration that the cultural cargo becomes stale and musty, yet the final reward to the steadfast community that maintains its cultural supremacy intact to the end is proportionately great. By degrees the subject-peoples, and even the barbarians themselves, become weary of the prevailing uncertainty, the continual bickerings and petty warfare of a state of anarchy, and long for the ordered security and peace of former civilization. In their despair they seek everywhere for guidance and leadership in the re-establishment of civilization. It is then that they find the cultural minority, the 'Ark,' that has survived the destruction of the past, and gladly submit themselves to the authority of these last possessors of cultural inspiration, and follow them blindly. As the 'robot' automatons in Capek's play, R.U.R., submitted themselves and all their usurped powers to the last human being in the hope of his restoring the lost knowledge of procreation, so have the peoples of the barbaric ages submitted themselves to the last civilized beings in the hope of their restoring the lost arts of civilization.

The first obvious and essential duty of dawning autocracy is to subject the surrounding barbarian peoples to authority and extend the domains of civilization to embrace a large united empire. In fact, the autocratic phase is essentially a military phase, and one of the outstanding features is a large standing army, which is ever prepared to defend the community from attack and undertake the conquest of further territories for the occupation and exploitation of the new civilized community.

The New Empire in Egypt, Assyria, and the Mogul Empire in India were all absolute military states in which the standing army played the most important role of all. The Ming dynasty also gathered together the flower of the fighting men of China to expel the Mongol barbarians and restore Chinese independence.

The military organization of Peru was remarkably efficient, being turned to the deliberate conquest of the surrounding Indian tribes, extending the Inca Empire for hundreds of miles up and down the Andes. The Janissaries of the Turkish Empire were, perhaps, the most famous standing army of recent history. Even the Papacy possessed its standing army in the form of the knightly orders of the Middle Ages dedicated to the service of Christendom against the Saracens and the Heathen.

Autocratic government of a vast empire cannot be exercised by the absolute ruler personally without aid, despite all preconceptions to the contrary. The autocrat is compelled to delegate local authority and minor details of administrations to officials and assistants, who form an immense bureaucratic instrument of government. As autocratic rule is centralized and despotic, this bureaucratic regime is a vital feature and enters into the lives of the people at every point, ordering their affairs in every detail, and exacting an absolute obedience to authority. Indeed, all the cultural powers of the entire civilization are in this phase centred in the autocratic court and the bureaucracy.

The Political Cycle

The officials of the government are generally the only members of the community capable of reading and writing, and were on this account known in early times by the general title of 'scribes.'

The scribes of Assyria are frequently mentioned in the Bible, and the activities of the Assyrian bureaucracy were on such a vast scale that whole national communities were actually transported in huge enforced migrations from one part of the empire to another, as, for example, the Jews to Babylon and the Samaritans into Palestine.

In Peru an equally powerful bureaucracy held sway under the Inca, and similar large-scale exchanges of population were undertaken. The autocracy of early China produced a bureaucratic system of government remarkable for its elaboration and complexity, which is fully described in the books of the 'Chou-li' dating from 1100 B.C.

The Sultanate found the Ulema or learned clergy of Islam invaluable as a source of officials for the efficient administration of the vast Turkish Empire.

The Papacy itself was the head of a highly efficient bureaucracy, within which home affairs were watched over by the bishops, education was maintained by the monasteries, poor relief was in the hands of the nunneries, foreign affairs delegated to missionaries. Added to all this, a large body of enthusiastic clergy formed an army of officials, ever at the call of the papal Government, holding records of births, death, and marriages, accounts of property for the collection of tithes - indeed, just such a bureaucracy as today forms the modern state.

Autocratic bureaucracy differs in several important particulars from the government of later empire. Office is never restricted to one race or caste, although adherence to the state religion is a necessary condition. Herein lies the vital distinction from the later caste administration of imperial oligarchy. The difference of autocratic bureaucracy from democratic administration lies not so much in the election of modern democratic officials, as the principle of election is a comparatively recent and Western invention, it is an essential matter of law. An autocracy knows no state of law: it is not restricted by the existence of a constitution. Its whole policy may at a moment's notice be entirely altered by imperial decree. The bureaucracy exists solely to convey the commands of the supreme ruler to his subjects: and the latter have no rights of any kind to which they might apply for protection against the occasional tyrannies of government. In the autocratic phase the state as expressed by the governmental bureaucracy is the be-all and end-all of civilization: the people only exist to the glorification of government and the service of the state. The idea that the state is the servant of the people is a later degenerate conception fostered by democracy, and much further from a realization of the truth of a higher superorganic reality in civilization.

It is an essential conclusion that the conception of civilization as a superorganism involves the mortality of civilization, and as inevitably its growth and decline. No organism is static: it changes imperceptibly from day to day, and markedly from year to year. Although the cultural superorganism has a lifetime of between two and three thousand years, and its rate of growth is slow, yet as the centuries pass a marked change in social and political organization becomes evident. As in the case of human beings, it is impossible to make allowance for the ever-changing inner character of the organism. For long periods one outward political and social form must be maintained, despite the unceasing growth of the superorganism. The autocratic phase is the 'school' of civilization, when the community is subjected to an absolute discipline, and taught the lost arts of bygone days, or the newborn inspiration of contemporary genius. Indeed, the resemblance to 'schooldays' is remarkable, when the bureaucracy forms the 'teaching staff,' the autocrat the 'headmaster,' and implicit obedience is the order of the times. But school life is notoriously a makeshift in the youthful period of life, and although admirably adapted to the boy of say twelve to fifteen, the absolute discipline of the school system comes harshly to the child of less than ten, newly come from the individual care of his mother, and is felt as a grievous restriction upon his freedom of action by a youth of seventeen and upwards. Exactly so is the experience of society under autocracy. As the primitive peoples are dragged up from their barbaric individualism under the sway of autocratic rule the harsh discipline chafes upon them, but later, in the intermediate stage of youthful culture, almost perfect acquiescence with authority is felt. However, as dawning maturity changes the character of civilized society, the strong central government is found an unbearable check upon individual national genius, and provincial revolt against the autocrat follows. Just as the youth before leaving school feels an ever-increasing impatience with the leading strings of school discipline, so society gradually becomes embittered against autocratic authority; but society cannot 'leave school.' When society has reached the stage of having outgrown the 'school' of autocracy, that 'school' must be destroyed, its autocrat 'headmaster' deposed, its bureaucratic 'staff' dispersed, its military 'canes' broken: then the dawning of manhood of civilization may be attained. Civilization has come of age.

The Political Cycle

We have already noted that in a state of autocracy all culture is in the hands of the bureaucracy, as in the lower classes of a school the only learned individuals are the masters. By degrees, however, culture passes from the metropolis and the bureaucracy to the provinces and the higher ranks of the people. Culture is no longer a monopoly of government; as in the upper classes of a school the scholars themselves have become learned and sometimes most tactlessly surpass their teachers. With the spread of culture to the more intelligent grades of society, the task of government becomes increasingly difficult. Gradually the spontaneous obedience so unreservedly offered at one time to authority is withdrawn, and force has to be applied more and more to maintain state discipline. Certain sections of the people are beginning to think for themselves, and no longer recognize the autocratic court and the bureaucracy as their cultural superiors. A disruptive tendency threatens to rend the fabric of the autocratic state.

Despite all compromise and reform, a point is finally reached when autocracy can no longer withstand the disruptive tendencies at work within society. This final destruction overtakes autocracy after a varying period of ascendancy, and a period of local provincial autonomy follows. Resistance to centralized autocracy has its origin in a general revulsion of the more sophisticated sections of the community against autocratic discipline and bureaucratic control, but a widespread diffused resistance of a social nature can never succeed in overturning the powerful centralized authority of the metropolis. It must of necessity find local centres of organization and local leaders before it can become effective. As yet only a very limited social caste have become cultivated beyond their fellows, and these combine together in provincial centres to set their united local powers against the international sway of the autocrat. Local leaders are chosen, and the remainder swear allegiance to them in the struggle with authority.

This is the origin of what can only be termed 'Nationalism.' Where several subject-nations and races exist, local resistance will naturally be organized to follow national and racial lines Even where there is little difference of race the local combinations adopted against autocratic authority will tend to intensify small differences of dialect and custom into national distinctions, forming national states from a comparatively uniform people. Disruption from the international empire of autocracy is thus best termed 'Nationalism,' even when no vital distinction of race is involved.

In early China the decline of the authority of the Chou emperors was so gradual that it is difficult to set a date to the independence of the many so-called 'Contending States' which arose in the provinces of the Chinese Empire.

Early Indian autocracy associated with Buddhism gave way to Brahmin noble disruption, when local Hindu rajas held sway in many independent principalities throughout India.

In Japan imperial authority and the actual possession of the landed estates of the realm passed from the hands of the autocratic Fujiwara shogunate to those of the Taira and Minamoto families of nobility, when the whole country lapsed for centuries into a disruptive conglomerate of local 'daimyos,' each fighting for his own land.

Finally in Europe the Reformation was a typical provincial revulsion against the autocratic sway of Pope and Emperor, and gave birth to the national states of Europe from the former united empire of Christendom.

Following upon the disruption of the provinces from centralized government, a local form of administration must be established to replace that of the former imperial bureaucracy. The only type of administration yet known to civilization is the centralized government of autocracy, and inevitably this must form the initial model for the government of the new national states. Hence the leaders of provincial revolt, when they have gained their independence of autocracy, form absolute monarchies, which reproduce on a miniature scale the original autocratic state. There is the same despotic authority, concentration of local economic resources, and also a similar bureaucratic organization of government. In a modified degree almost all the functions of autocracy already traced may be applied to monarchy on a small scale.

There is, however, a vital distinction. As already noted, the primary cause of revolt against autocracy is the advancing culture of a section of the subject-peoples of the empire. These superior individuals only choose one of their number as leader, and submit to his authority as monarch, because of the necessity of an organized resistance to combat autocratic suppression and maintain national independence against the rivalry of other national states. The elevation of the monarch to his supreme position is, however, only granted on condition of his furthering and maintaining the superior caste. This caste accordingly monopolizes the bureaucratic positions under the monarchic Government, and the positions of command in the monarchic armies, without regard for the possible abilities of members of the lower, not yet cultured, classes. Monarchy rules, not like autocracy through a bureaucracy of talent drawn on account of ability from all sections of the community, but through a bureaucracy of nobility drawn on account of birth and breeding from one cultural caste. Although the authority of the monarch is still absolute, on the model of that of the former autocrat, he is restricted in the exercise of his authority by the necessity of respecting the rights and privileges of the noble caste, while the autocrat had no need to consider the interests of anyone beyond his own.

In India the highest Brahman caste, after the decline of Buddhism, took the lead as a cultivated priesthood in the administration of the independent Raja states.

Later again, after an intermediate period of Moslem democracy and Mogul autocracy, they came to the front once more as the administrators of the Mahratta states.

The 'Literati' of ancient China took a leading part in the government of the 'Contending States,' Confucius himself seeking in all parts of China for the 'perfect prince' who should put his political theories to practical use.

The 'Samurai' of Japan were no less illustrious as the administrators and defenders of the Daimyo principalities into which Japan relapsed for so many centuries.

In Europe, similarly, every one of the national states that arose out of the Reformation developed a privileged caste of nobility and gentry who asserted an absolute monopoly of government office and land ownership.

In more advanced civilizations, such as the ancient Mediterranean and modern Levantine, hereditary monarchy is abandoned, as the hereditary principle is recognized as erroneous and even dangerous. In its place a tyranny or dictatorship gives power to the really able man who arises in the state, while in the possible interregnum of a lack of supreme ability a temporary oligarchic council maintains the political continuity.

Greek history is interspersed with the advent of 'tyrants' who ruled the city states with absolute disregard of constitutional restrictions.

Latin America is famous or notorious for the many 'dictators' who have directed the government of its republics.

Civilization As Divine Superman

Today the nationalist states of Southern Europe and the Levant supply startling modern examples of absolute dictatorship by obscure men of pre-eminent ability.

It is one of the most common and dangerous errors made by modern Europeans to assume that war is an inevitable part of international politics. In the nationalist phase of cultural disruption war may be an inevitable feature of civilization, but only in this one phase, which has been entirely unknown in some few civilizations and of short duration in others. The profound peace that prevailed in the Roman Empire earned the title Pax Romana, and this state of internal peace is much more usual in World History than a perennial state of war. Nationalism breeds war with an inevitable certainty that is horrifying. While an autocracy is principally concerned in maintaining an efficient defence against barbarians and other enemies, and only embarks upon wars of conquest upon due consideration of the cost, national states are apparently driven into war by an inner urge. Furthermore, war for the people of an autocratic empire is a distant affair waged upon some remote frontier, but for the people of a small national state it means intimate danger to life and limb as well as unending damage to personal property. War reserves its worst terrors for the nationalist phase of internecine conflict, for then war is not an intercultural contest, but in reality a civil war within the bounds of one cultural system.

From the point of view of the superorganic conception of civilization war following the disruption of autocracy is an inevitable outcome. Disruption from the original unity of autocratic government can only be a passing phase in the life-course of the superorganism. It is caused by the necessity of freeing the elements of culture arising in the whole community from the restrictions of centralized autocratic discipline: but once this end has been attained the superorganism strives to recover once more the natural unity of culture. This unity can only be gained in a national system of independent states by the conquest of all the others by the most powerful state or by the invasion of some more virile semi-barbaric people from the borders of civilization. In order that the 'hegemony' of the cultural system may be attained, and cultural unity restored, each national state is embued with the utmost patriotism and ambition, so that it endeavours to extend its influence and power at the expense of its neighbours, while maintaining its own independence unimpaired at all costs. Hence the interminable internecine struggle that marks the nationalist phase in every civilization, until one nation or semi-barbaric people gains the ascendancy or democratic revolution finally overtakes oligarchic society. As each state is determined to defend its own independence, any threatening ascendancy on the part of any one nation will be resisted to the last by a confederation of the others and alliances to maintain the 'balance of power' will be made. Hence the actual attainment of a hegemony is exceedingly difficult, and in some civilizations never accomplished before the advent of democratic empire.

India during Brahman ascendency, following the decline of central Buddhist autocracy, was a conglomerate of rival Raja states, which being ever engaged in violent internecine warfare, rose and fell in individual power, without any one state gaining the permanent hegemony of the peninsula.

The Contending States of Ancient China, the city states of Ancient Greece, and the national states of Modern Europe bear a remarkable resemblance. In each case, out of an initial chaos of numberless independent principalities, three great powers emerged by the conquest and absorption of their neighbours. In China, Ts'in, Ch'u, and Ts'i; in Greece, Sparta, Thebes, and Athens; in Europe, Germany, France, and Britain. Furthermore, in each civilization the most powerful state attempted in a 'Great War' to gain the hegemony of civilization—in China, Ts'in; in Greece, Athens; in Europe, Germany—only to be met by an alliance of all the other powers. Ts'in was actually successful despite the valiant resistance of the other Chinese states led by Ch'u. It is said that in the final battles hundreds of thousands took part, giving this early struggle quite the character of a 'Great War.' It is unnecessary to recall the failure of Athens in the Peloponnesian War, or of Germany in the recent war, to gain that hegemony, which undoubtedly inspired the heroic efforts of both nations.

Although the national communities may not appreciate the actual final goal of hegemony to which their patriotic efforts tend, yet that is the aim of the superorganic spirit of civilization. The recovery of cultural unity is the first and foremost purpose, and mere national peace and prosperity must be sacrificed to this great end. The many independent local states of the period immediately following the disruption of autocracy are gradually conquered and absorbed by a handful of 'great powers,' and then one or another of these makes the great effort towards 'hegemony,' only to be resisted to the death by an alliance of the others. The nationalism and patriotism of these independent states constitute an inner urge towards war, regardless of the advantage or disadvantage of war in itself. Consciously or unconsciously the individual national states follow the instinct of restoring the unity of culture by each establishing its own individual ascendancy over all other nations as the cultural leader of civilization.

War is the inevitable outcome of such conflicting interests, where one nation alone may attain the eventual supremacy.

2. The Oligarchic Phase

The middle period of civilization is first and foremost the epoch of caste ascendancy. Culture has spread from the original autocratic centre of civilization to the more intelligent and sophisticated members of the community throughout its wide domain. This body of newly enlightened individuals inspires revolt against centralization, and aids the establishment of local monarchies, to gain a less oppressive form of government, and to give effect to the diffusion of culture geographically and socially. In their attitude to the less-cultured classes of the community the newly cultured display those attributes which are universally associated with 'caste.' Just as the autocracy resists the spread of culture to the upper classes of the people, so does this new oligarchy resist the sophistication and self-assertion of the 'common' people. As men in authority throughout the life-course of civilization resist the inevitable advance of events, so do the cultured oligarchs attempt to stabilize and perpetuate their own supremacy by every means at their disposal. For a time, even for centuries, they are almost entirely successful: and a form of society is established which from the purely cultural point of view represents the highest level to which civilization can attain. Indeed, the oligarchic phase may be represented as the 'university' training of civilization in art for art's sake before the serious life-work of subjugating nature by practical and material means is undertaken.

The oligarchy maintains its supremacy over the common people in a rather unexpected and very effective manner. 'Caste' is simply a matter of 'birth.' It would seem that mankind has at all times and throughout the globe appreciated the evolutionary value of selective breeding; indeed, from the moment man began to domesticate the animals this principle could not fail to become evident. In any case, oligarchy deliberately attempts to maintain its cultural superiority by the prevention of the breeding of the select few with the common herd of the uncultivated. In point of fact, a restriction of this sort will only maintain the original stock unimpaired in purity, but will not in itself involve any betterment of this stock—rather it raises great risk of degeneration through excessive inbreeding. But after all from a political point of view the main object of caste is to prevent the spread of the divine inspiration of culture from the oligarchy to the people as a whole, rather than the betterment of the superior caste as such.

The fetish of birth 'and breeding' is only a means of attaining this end. Regulations as to marriage are therefore the main features and principal support of 'caste,' and a true 'oligarchy,' in the sense of a higher class of cultured individuals, can be readily distinguished from any other body of men by this one feature of the restriction of marriage within the caste. Very simply the general caste regulation is that marriages within the caste are alone legal, and their offspring legitimate caste members. Any children a high-caste man may have with a low-caste woman are illegitimate, and will not normally be admitted to the caste, while any sexual intercourse between a high-caste woman, married or unmarried, with a man of the lower orders is punishable with the utmost severity. In some civilizations these marriage regulations are given absolute legal form, and it would be difficult to find any oligarchic system where they are not reflected in the legal code. In more advanced civilizations they are a part of the even more potent unwritten law of society, and are enforced by the dread weapon of social ostracism.

In India the Brahmans, as the highest Hindu caste, have maintained immense social privileges ever since the decline of Buddhism and the rise of the Hindu Raja states. Today India is the most caste-ridden land of the world, with the British crowning the pyramid of society as the 'super-caste' dominating the whole.

In Central America the Maya noble caste was maintained by strict marriage regulations, such that any noble who married a low-caste woman was automatically reduced to her rank.

In Europe each nation has developed a higher caste bearing a distinctive title—in England 'gentleman,' in France 'noblesse,' in Spain 'caballero,' in Germany 'Adel.' Although actual legal restriction of marriage to the superior class has scarcely been established anywhere in Europe, yet the unwritten law of society has discouraged, and often practically debarred, marriage beneath the social station of the caste to any of its members.

In China the descendants of the first philosophers and teachers, who guided the rulers of the Contending States through the storms of civil war, formed families of 'Literati,' who gradually gained a monopoly of 'mandarin' positions of state, and held the proud position of a higher caste of accumulated culture.

In Japan was developed the magnificent caste of the Samurai as hereditary warriors, with a very high code of honour. Originally attached to the Daimyos as bodyguards, they rapidly developed a corporate independent existence and maintained their purity of birth with scrupulous care, while avoiding all degrading occupations.

Greek citizenship depended at all times upon both paternal and maternal descent, insuring the continuity of pure birth.

In South America pure blood Spanish descent is still the only passport to social ascendancy, and hence to political power.

An imperial caste system may be arrived at in civilization direct from autocracy, without intermediate disruption into a nationalist system. This is impossible to the super-organism in itself by any spontaneous action, as the revolt from autocracy must take a disruptive form. On the other hand, civilization passes through an exceedingly critical period in the decline of autocratic government, when the people begin to withhold their obedience to central authority, and local monarchic centres are not yet developed as alternative objects of patriotic sentiment. At this time the civilized community is exceedingly vulnerable to external invasion, as there is a complete lack of corporate sentiment in civilization which can form an inspiration to imperial defence. The invader may be a semi-barbaric people from the borders of civilization, or an oligarchic caste drawn from a neighbouring civilization. While the civilized community will resist to the death invasion and destruction by an absolutely barbarian people, it is prepared to acquiesce in the deposition of centralized autocracy by a semi-barbaric people or a caste of foreign culture, as it anticipates from the invader a more tolerable and enlightened form of government.

In the time of the Ming the Manchu Tatars took advantage of a state of rebellion in China to overrun the country. They established one of the most perfect oligarchies in the world, living in special settlements, such as the famous Tatar city in Pekin, and forbidding all intermarriage with the subject-Chinese.

Mediterranean and European civilizations have both accomplished the conquest of another cultural system. The Greeks conquered the Persians, and the British, the Moguls. From the first the Greeks in Mesopotamia and the British in India were essentially a mercantile caste and their settlements a network of commercial organization. By degrees, however, they were both compelled to undertake the administration of the subject-peoples, and founded many new cities as the centres of their rule, such as Alexandria, Antiochia, and Seleucia; Bombay, Madras, and Calcutta. The basic condition of marriage restriction is as strongly apparent in British India as in the Greek communities of Mesopotamia, where Greek descent on both sides was the criterion of citizenship. The one unforgivable crime in India is marriage with the native.

The oligarchic state of civilization can only develop fully in a united empire, such as those formed by foreign conquest. Under nationalist disruption oligarchy is disunited and hence at a disadvantage. However, many national systems are finally transformed into imperial systems by the attainment of a 'hegemony' by one or another of the states, when a general imperial oligarchy is established. As has been already pointed out, the very strong, almost religious, sentiment of 'patriotism' tends to encourage internecine war between the national states with the gradual elimination of the weaker and the survival of the stronger as 'great powers.' These great powers then engage in a last supreme struggle for the ultimate supremacy.

In the case of many civilizations, as, for example, in Europe, the weaker states contrive by a system of alliances to maintain the 'balance of power,' and prevent the supremacy of any one state, in this case Germany. In the majority of cases, however, a 'hegemony' is finally attained, generally by an outlying semi-barbaric state of greater virility.

In Egypt, after the fall of the Rameses in 1090 B.C., the whole country relapsed into a number of warring principalities, until the semi-barbaric Ethiopians fought their way down the Nile and united the whole valley into one imperial system once more.

In Greece, Athens, Sparta, and Thebes in turn attempted to gain the hegemony, only to be frustrated by the alliance of the other weaker states against the dominant power of the moment. It was left to the semi-barbaric Macedonia of the north to complete the conquest of the Greek states and lead the united Greek peoples against Persia.

In ancient China, as we have seen, Ts'in gained a hegemony over the many other Contending States, and the King of Ts'in became the 'First Universal Emperor' of all China. In Japan the three great statesmen, Nobunaga, Hideyoshi, and Iyeyasu, raised one small fief among the many Daimyo principalities to supreme power, founding the Tokugawa shogunate. Even in Mexico the Aztecs were just completing the conquest of the remaining Central American states when the Spaniards brought the whole native civilization tottering down to destruction.

Civilization As Divine Superman

Once 'hegemony' is established in civilization, either by the elimination contest of nationalist warfare or by the introduction of a foreign caste of conquerors, cultural unity is restored, but the superorganism does not rest contented with this desirable event, it embarks upon an ambitious project of foreign conquest. It is, indeed, during the period of imperialist oligarchy that civilization accomplishes its greatest expansion. In autocracy the state is mainly concerned in maintaining its existence in the flood of external and internal barbarism: the national states are entirely preoccupied with the task of defending their own independence, and seeking to establish a hegemony over their neighbours within the existing civilization: but the united imperial oligarchy is free to apply its excess energies to the expansion of the superorganism on a large scale. This policy of extending the area, and the population, ruled over by the oligarchic caste is what is generally termed 'Imperialism.' In the case of civilizations that have direct access to large land areas not as yet cultivated, it takes the form of the general expansion of empire to the utmost practicable limits. In civilizations more limited by physical boundaries it frequently takes the form of the formation of colonies overseas, or the conquest of foreign cultural systems.

The Han dynasty that followed the Ts'in on the imperial throne spread Chinese authority not only through Southern China to the Burmese mountains, but over the entire vast area of Central Asia as far as the shores of the Caspian. The Greeks, united by Macedonian conquest, voluntarily elected Alexander 'captain-general' of their expedition for the conquest of Persia and Egypt. Hideyoshi of Japan immediately took advantage of the restoration of Japanese imperial unity to launch the Samurai caste of warriors on no less ambitious a project than the invasion and conquest of China by way of Korea. He was only frustrated after great initial successes by the loss of the command of the seas.

Although the land hegemony of Europe has never been accomplished, England attained the command or 'hegemony' of the seas from Holland and France over a century ago, and has since embarked upon a worldwide policy of colonization and conquest, of which the occupation of India was only a part.

Inevitably with the restoration of a united empire in civilization a centralized form of government must be reintroduced. A new bureaucracy must arise on the lines of the administration of autocratic empire. A difference, however, at once becomes apparent, for on no account does the bureaucracy of oligarchic empire become the be-all and end-all of civilization, as it does in the autocratic phase. Culture is no longer the exclusive monopoly of the government, and the newly arisen cultured class of the oligarchy must be taken into account. The administration is not only exercised by a bureaucracy exclusively recruited from the superior caste, but for the first time the theory of government as a form of public service begins to arise. The emperor as such is no longer an absolute despot, whose merest word is a binding decree, he is rather the representative of the oligarchy, who gives a united central authority to the ordinances necessary to the well-being of the superior caste. There is as yet no thought of ruling for the benefit of the whole people, but the maintenance of the interests and privileges of the oligarchy is the first and foremost duty of government.

'Law,' as a new conception of static government regulation, begins to develop. Under autocracy 'law,' if it may be so termed, merely consisted of 'standing orders' to the bureaucracy instructing them how to deal with matters of small importance in the ordinary routine of government, which were not worth referring to the capital. These 'standing orders' might be withdrawn or altered at the will of the autocrat, and formed no guarantee to the people of a uniform administration: furthermore, the autocrat always reserved the right of making individual exceptions to the regulations, he had laid down for guidance, at his own discretion. The oligarchic caste, however, refuse thus to be at the mercy of every whim of imperial government, and are at pains to define certain rights and privileges which are the inalienable perquisites of their class. This is the beginning of 'law' as such, which has a permanent real existence as a check upon the vagaries of absolute government, and a definition of the rights of the individual, in this first stage those of the oligarch. The lower orders are as yet outside the laws. They possess few rights, if any, and are subject to the most brutal criminal code for offences against their superiors.

Greek law defined the rights and privileges of Greek citizenship with great care, but slaves and foreigners, 'hoi polloi' generally, were outside its province.

In India, the Hindu code maintained the privileges of the high-caste Brahman and suppressed the Sudra, treating with great lenience offences offered by members of higher castes towards those of lower, and with great severity similar offences offered by members of the lower castes towards their superiors.

In Europe itself a brutal criminal code was enforced against the lower classes up to within recent times, and, furthermore, a code which was, at least in England, deprived by the privilege of 'Benefit of Clergy' of an equal severity towards the upper classes.

Defence in the case of an oligarchy is a twofold problem. On the one hand, the ever-present barbarian enemies of civilization must be kept at bay, and on the other hand the dominant caste must be maintained against the revolt of the common or subject people. These considerations are further complicated by the fact that the imperialist urge to expansion calls for large armies to undertake the conquest of new provinces abroad. The solutions arrived at have depended upon the conditions of the time. Where the oligarchy has been a native caste of higher culture it has generally been sufficient to use armies of soldiers recruited from the lower orders, but officered exclusively by the upper classes. This has also been the method generally adopted by the independent oligarchic states during the nationalist phase.

In Europe this principle has been illustrated most clearly when three stages of noble descent were a condition of holding a commission in the armies of the national monarchy in France, when the army of the modern German Empire was officered exclusively from the upper class, and when even in England during the national crisis of the recent war public schoolboys were commissioned and sent out to France to command veteran troops without the slightest practical experience of war.

In other civilizations service in the army has been the valued privilege of the superior caste, making quite certain of the subjection of the common people to the dominant oligarchy. Among the Greeks, military service was one of the most treasured privileges of citizenship. The Japanese Samurai based their caste superiority purely upon their military tradition. The Kshatriyas in India, second only in caste to the administrative Brahmans, were soldiers, and possessed the exclusive privilege of military service to the Hindu rajas.

Those nations which have accomplished the conquest of a foreign civilization have found it necessary to maintain a strong striking force of their own race, as well as a native militia, to maintain their racial supremacy.

The Greeks in Persia maintained themselves by sheer military power, and were still known in India in 150 B.C., two hundred years after Alexander, as the 'viciously valiant Yonas.'

The Political Cycle

The Manchus in China were careful to maintain beside the native militia a hereditary army descended from the original army of conquest, whose Manchu soldiery were known as 'Bannermen' and housed in splendour in the Tartar settlements.

The English in India uphold their authority and undertake the defence of the country by means of a force of regular British troops, supplemented by a larger number of natives officered by British. These latter, termed 'sepoys,' make excellent soldiers, but obviously must not be allowed to exceed a manageable proportion of the regular British troops. Neglect of this obvious precaution was the primary cause of the terrible Indian Mutiny of the 1850's, when the proportion of native to British troops was allowed to rise to as high as seven to one, instead of the three to one of present Indian policy.

In course of time, just as culture spread from autocracy to the higher classes of the people, despite all endeavours of the government to prevent education passing beyond the bureaucracy of administration, so it spreads as inevitably further from the oligarchic caste to the lower orders in general. As the people as a whole become more sophisticated they are no longer content to leave all political power in the hands of the upper class, and more definitely they become increasingly unwilling to submit to the appropriation of their entire surplus production to cater to the luxurious tastes of the privileged few. The authority of the oligarchs like that of the autocracy before them gradually wanes, as the people withhold the obedience formerly rendered them with such absolute good will. A growing unrest threatens the existence of the caste regime.

Returning to the analogy of human life as an explanation of the life-course of the cultural superorganism, we find that the oligarchic period with its insistence upon the superiority of pure culture is reminiscent of 'university' life. Just as the schoolboy escapes from the strict discipline of schooldays to the comparative freedom of university life, so does civilization escape from the centralized authority of autocracy to the greater freedom of oligarchy. University life, however, cannot last for ever, not because of expense and the need of earning a living so much, as because the pursuit of pure culture does not satisfy the practical instincts of the average man. Having learned what there is to 'know,' he wishes to apply this knowledge in finding things to 'do.' In the case of civilization the process is very similar. At first civilization is willing to apply a large part of its energies to the pursuit of knowledge and pure culture, and to apportion its rewards to the cultivated few, who are capable of showing the way to their attainment. After a time, however, the period of study becomes too prolonged, and civilization seeks an opportunity to apply its accumulated knowledge to the material realization of economic progress for the benefit of the people as a whole. A new basis of social organization is sought, when the ability to promote the economic progress and emancipation of the community is the criterion of success, and not the ability to amass personal culture and preserve the privileges of a caste. So it is when the young man goes down from his university to take part in business life. He is no longer asked, 'What do you know?' but 'What can you do?' But the civilized community cannot 'go down' from the 'university' of the oligarchic phase: it is compelled to depose its privileged caste of 'dons,' to degrade its officer corps of 'proctors,' by a social revolution of greater or less intensity, before it can enter into the economic emancipation of the democratic phase.

Democratic institutions may be introduced without proletarian revolution by a benevolent ruler. Here it must be fully understood that the term 'democracy' as used in this discussion does not necessarily mean that government is exercised or even controlled by the people themselves, but it does mean that the government is organized and directed to the 'benefit' of the people as a whole, just as 'oligarchy' means government for the benefit of a restricted caste, and 'autocracy' government for the benefit of the autocrat and his immediate court alone. The idea of the whole people electing their representatives to form a government is a modern development which depends very largely upon the improved communications of modern times, which make it possible for the whole people to act in unison. In the ancient democratic empires the difficulty and slowness of imperial communications made it impossible for the whole people to express their will with sufficient swiftness in times of emergency, and hence they were forced to delegate authority to comparatively despotic but benevolent rulers.

Twice during the long history of Egypt benevolent Pharaohs organized the imperial administration for the benefit of the people as a whole. Shortly before the collapse of the Early Egyptian civilization to the invasion of the Hyksos, the XII dynasty from Thebes established a regime which, although despotic in form, was highly benevolent in effect, bearing the greatest possible contrast to the former autocratic, self-centred rule of the Pharaohs of Memphis. Over a thousand years later the regime of the last native Pharaohs at Memphis before the conquest of the Persians was no less enlightened.

In early Mesopotamia, Hammurabi of Babylon led the subject people of his obscure city against the foreign domination of the Elamite caste, and united Babylonia under his enlightened sway, publishing his famous code of equal laws.

Similarly, Yang Kien, who founded the Suy-Tang Empire, published an improved code of laws on a democratic basis.

Mahomet himself introduced a new principle of the democratic equality of all 'Believers' before Allah, and as despot of Medina laid the foundations of the great democratic empire of Islam.

A very special case must not be overlooked in India, where the Moslems from Afghanistan and Persia conquered the Hindus, and attempted to impose Islamic ideals of democratic equality upon the Hindu social system.

Although the introduction of democratic institutions for the benefit of the people as a whole has more generally been the work of some great benevolent ruler, who has thereby enlisted the interests of the common people in his service, yet later civilizations have frequently produced examples of popular revolt against oligarchic supremacy, which has taken a purely republican form being almost spontaneously furthered by the whole people in unison.

In Rome, which was originally organized on much the same lines as the Greek city states, the 'plebeians,' or non-citizens, rose in revolt against the 'patricians,' and compelled the latter to admit them not only to equal political rights, but, still more important, to 'connubium.'

In modern English times, the English revolution of the Puritans against the Stuarts and their cavalier supporters was finally suppressed after it had run its course, but as large numbers of the Puritan revolutionaries migrated to America, the eventual revolt of the American colonies against the home country was a sequel to the democratic tendencies of the Commonwealth.

The revolutions of France and Russia are too well known to need any special mention. Also, in the Far East, the revolution of the Japanese people, overturning the privileges of the Samurai, is interesting, paralleled as it is by the Chinese revolution deposing the Manchus.

A certain transitory period marks the advent of democracy. Revolution is not achieved overnight, and an oligarchic form of government may survive in the most unexpected forms. Pure democratic equality is only attained after the violent agitation of revolution has been calmed. There is a very distinct tendency on the part of the revolutionaries to institute themselves as a new exclusive, if benevolent, oligarchy in charge of affairs, and this oligarchic direction of revolution tends to degenerate into a normal exploitation of the masses to the advantage of the governing minority. Revolution places supreme power in the hands of a new group, which may profess benevolent intentions, but which falls easily into the temptation to use its usurped powers in the traditional manner to its own personal benefit. Such 'inverted' oligarchies have been :

- The Senators in Rome.

- The Medinians in the early Caliphate.

- The Jacobins in the French Revolution.

- The Bolsheviks in the Russian Revolution.

- The 'Elder Statesmen' in Japan.

- The Kuo Min Tang in China.

During the whole course of Moslem Empire at Delhi in India the Moslem community never rose above the level of a minority revolutionary regime exploiting the Hindus for its own benefit.

In America, the southern planters, who had taken the leading part in the ejection of the British, formed a minority in control of federal government after the Revolution.

The outbreak of revolution, or the introduction of benevolent democratic institutions, generally takes place in some provincial urban centre or national state, and inflames the violent resistance of the established oligarchic order throughout civilization, which sees in this democratic idealism the most dangerous threat to its continued existence. Long before the local movement has the aspect of a material international force, the oligarchic order is everywhere fully alarmed and aroused, and proceeds with all the powers at its command to attempt the suppression of the local democracy as the dangerous source of a subversive doctrine. Where united empire has been established by oligarchy the resistance of the oligarchic order to local democratic revolt is only to be expected, but the fact that hostile states in a disruptive nationalist system forget their traditional rivalries in a general alliance against that state, which introduces democratic institutions, is less to be expected. The danger of the infection of revolution passing to their own peoples awakens the neighbouring states to the seriousness of the existence of revolution in the common fabric of civilization, as a threat to the supremacy of the oligarchic order in general, and they unite in active antagonism to the revolutionary regime. Hence the advent of local revolution is sufficient to cause the national states to unite in one common international policy, and as long as the danger threatens an unprecedented unanimity holds sway in international affairs. Yet all the united pressure of the rest of civilization is insufficient to accomplish the suppression of local revolution, and the local democratic community triumphs almost miraculously over its enemies in the very moment of apparent extinction. The idealist spirit of democracy proves inextinguishable, and the very armies of the oligarchs are secretly in sympathy with the democratic principles of the community they have been commanded to suppress.

Rome survived an alliance of Phoenicians and Greeks, the great mercantile peoples of the Mediterranean, even when Hannibal marched an army into Italy and ravaged the peninsula for more than ten years.

Although Mahomet actually had the temerity to send letters to the great emperors of his day calling upon them to embrace the 'true' Islamic faith, he escaped an expedition sent by the outraged Persian government to arrest him.

The measures taken by the English Government to effect the subjection of the rebellious colonies in America were very similar to those used by Hannibal against Rome, and English armies, largely composed of German mercenaries, marched up and down the American coast-lands for several years. Yet the colonists maintained their resistance to English authority until the English, like the Carthaginians, were compelled to evacuate their forces.

The coalitions of the European powers against the French Revolution were remarkable both for their immense display of force and their complete failure to effect their object. Repeatedly, when the Jacobin regime seemed doomed, a desperate patriotic effort brought the allied advance to a standstill. Valmy was symbolic of the hopelessness of subjecting democratic revolution by force of arms.

The present Russian Revolution has gone through the same stage, when the Central European and Allied powers forgot their bitter enmities in a common hostility to Bolshevism. Yet, although the Germans were in Finland, the Baltic states, and the Ukraine, the British in Archangel, the French in Odessa, the Japanese in Vladivostock, and 'White' reactionaries in arms on all sides, the Russian Revolution proved irrepressible, and the foreigners were compelled to beat an undignified retreat.

In China, Canton has been the traditional centre of democratic revolt for generations, and every effort was made by the northern Tuchuns to capture the southern city and repress democracy once and for all. Yet, despite the fact that foreign subsidies were freely at the disposal of her enemies, Canton survived as the focus of Chinese Revolution.

The failure of the oligarchic order to crush the democratic community at the outset of revolution actually seals the doom of the caste regime. Offensive operations against the revolutionaries pass rapidly into a desperate defensive in an endeavour to prevent the expansion of the democratic state, while the spread of propaganda continually undermines the popular support of oligarchic government. For a time an uneasy state of apparent stability ensues, when revolution is apparently restricted to the local centre of revolt. This intermediate period may last for a varying time, but steadily by slow and almost imperceptible degrees democratic idealism is spreading in the form of propaganda throughout the civilized community, and popular resistance to oligarchic supremacy arises on all sides. At last oligarchic governmental authority is reduced to a mere outward shell, which lacks all inward support, and a state of instability follows, which can only be compared to the instability of autocracy on the verge of national disruption. Just as autocracy in that critical state was particularly fragile, and open to foreign invasion, so does the oligarchic system readily fall to conquest.

When the original democratic state has ordered its internal affairs, when the inevitable disturbance of revolution has passed, the revolutionary community submits to one military leadership, and undertakes the conquest of a vast empire covering the whole domain of civilization. This conquest proves unexpectedly easy for the simple reason that the resistance of the majority of the neighbouring peoples is half-hearted, as they welcome the advent of the revolutionary armies as liberators from the oligarchic yoke. Many of the great conquerors of history owe their military reputations in large measure to the idealist force of democratic propaganda, which inspired their own armies and undermined the loyalty of their opponents.

The Political Cycle

Hammurabi of Babylon had no difficulty in conquering the whole of Mesopotamia and restoring a united empire under his benevolent sway.

After the defeat of Hannibal, Rome seemed to gain her empire in the basin of the Mediterranean without serious effort. Pompey and Caesar had comparatively little difficulty in persuading the peoples of the East and West to accept the Law and Order of Roman government.

The conquests of the Moslem armies through Mesopotamia to Central Asia, and along the coast of Northern Africa to Spain and Southern France, appear miraculous when we consider that the original Arabian source of revolution lay among a few desert tribes, who could lay no pretensions to being an organized state. Nothing but the idealism of Islamic brotherhood could have inspired such immense military successes.

In India, although Islam was never accepted by more than a small minority of the Hindu people, yet the rulers of Delhi managed to conquer the whole peninsula down to the southernmost point of the Deccan.

In this same connection, the conquest and expansion that carried the United States of America across the whole continent from Atlantic to Pacific are significant.

In modern Europe, the French Revolution was the direct cause and inspiration of the marvellous conquests of Napoleon. In the early stages of his career he was everywhere welcomed as the liberator of the 'conquered' populace from the oppression of their own oligarchic rulers. It was only later, when his 'victories' had turned his head, that Napoleon turned tyrant was no longer acceptable to the democratic sentiment of Europe, and his empire collapsed on the withdrawal of popular support.

In China, the general, Chang Kai Shek, has shown himself the Napoleon of the Far East, and has led the Cantonese revolutionaries to the conquest of the entire former empire, an area as large as Europe.

3. The Democratic Phase

Revolution introduces the ideals of 'liberte,' 'egalite,' 'fraternite,' to civilized society, and these principles are incorporated into democracy as a stable order of society. Here again it must be fully understood that by 'democracy' no particular form of government is indicated, but an idealist organization of the people as a whole. Frequently in history a democratic people has been ruled by a benevolent despot, just as most oligarchies are ruled by monarchs or dictators, and some autocracies by an 'oligarchic' council. Democracy in the form of an ever recurrent phase of civilization is, in fact, a particular state of society, in which certain ideals of liberty, equality, and brotherhood are exalted to guiding principles of social intercourse. 'Fraternite' as such is more in the nature of a pious religious precept than a practical aspect of democratic society. Indeed brotherly love is unfortunately little in evidence in the fierce competition of democratic life. While autocracy and oligarchy are at pains to protect the weaker members of the community in return for their implicit obedience to authority, democracy is too much inclined to exalt the strong at the expense of the weak, to neglect those that fall by the roadside in cold unconcern. No man is responsible and each is for himself. 'Egalite' as a social term is, unfortunately, ambiguous, as it can be interpreted by the extremist as a claim of equality of wealth and consumption for weak and strong, efficient and inefficient, wise and foolish. This interpretation is quite erroneous, as democracy never intended to establish an equality of reward. The equality in question is merely the opposite of privilege, equality of opportunity. Nature herself forbids equality of attainment. It is most important to bear this vital distinction in mind. Democracy destroys the privilege of caste, so that every man may at least in theory start with an equal chance of success. It will be shown later how this form of equality defeats its own object, because of the emphasis democracy lays upon the first great popular ideal. 'Liberte' is the real keystone of the democratic structure, the one ideal that inspires the people as a whole. Freedom from the cramping restrictions of autocratic authority; freedom from the unbearable cultural pretensions of aristocratic privilege; freedom for the common man of the people to develop his own personality. Liberty also to amass personal wealth without fear of dispossession in favour of an omnipotent autocrat or a privileged caste; liberty to advance from the lowest class of society to the highest; but also liberty to displace those above, trample those beneath, in the desperate struggle of democratic competition. Liberty indeed for the strong to oppress the weak, gangway for the efficient in a hard, cold world, where material success is the individual object of attainment.

The Political Cycle

The ideal democratic social organization that gives effect to the principles of liberty and equality can only be established when the temporary anomalies caused by revolution are removed. The revolutionary regime, which prolongs oligarchic privilege in a real or inverted form, must, however great its services to the cause of democracy, be deposed from its ascendant position. This struggle of the common people against their self-constituted liberators is one of the most interesting movements of history. The revolutionary regime is frequently, if by no means always, much too extremist for the establishment of real democratic conditions, but in every case there is a natural human tendency for that section, which has attained to the foremost position in the state through the violent events of revolution, to cling to the advantages that accrue from this ascendancy quite regardless of democratic principles. Invariably it has been necessary for some great popular leader to arise, before the people have been able to break the tyranny of the revolutionaries. Many of the greatest names in history have been associated with the popular revolt of democratic society against its former leaders.

It was Julius Caesar who overturned the oligarchic pretensions of the Roman Senate, checked 'carpet-bagging' extortion at the expense of the provinces, and gave citizens of empire outside the Roman metropolis a large measure of democratic emancipation. It was indeed on account of his democratic reforms that the Senatorial party plotted his assassination, only to be finally and completely crushed by his successor Augustus.

Similarly, in the Caliphate, the caliph Othman curbed the pretensions of the Medinians to a place of privilege in the new Islamic Empire and suffered assassination at their hands, only to be followed by Moamiya, the founder of the Omayyad dynasty, who took the drastic step of removing the Islamic capital to Damascus out of reach of Medinian influence.

At the present day, Chang Kai Shek has suppressed the extremists of the Cantonese Kuo Min Tang, and has removed the capital of democratic China from Canton to Nankin to escape from extremist violence.

The suppression of the Jacobin regime in France after the Revolution was the greatest service that Napoleon rendered the French people.

Democracy attains through conquest by the original revolutionary community to international empire embracing the whole extent of civilization. At first it is only the propaganda of democratic liberty and equality that unites the many diverse nations and races into one empire: but by degrees unity is made more real by a 'standardization' of all forms of civilized expression within the whole cultural domain. As might be expected in this standardization, the language, arts, and laws of the original democratic community take a leading place, but are subtly influenced by the exotic habits of other of the peoples that make up the imperial complex.

As time passes the absence of national boundaries, and the freedom of intercourse between all parts of the new democratic empire, favour standardization to such an extent that national and even racial distinctions tend to become submerged in the common characteristics of imperial democratic citizenship. In all parts of the empire, even to the most distant provinces, the same laws, customs, and habits hold good, and all subjects of the empire enjoy the bonds of a common citizenship. Standardization of this wholesale nature cannot be effected without considerable internal disturbance. It has already been noted that the political ascendancy of the revolutionary faction in the original focus of democratic revolt must be broken before widespread empire can be conquered: but the original democratic community as a whole remains for a long time in a position of supremacy in the empire. It is only by degrees that the trend of standardization brings the provincial peoples more and more into line with this original home country of democracy, and national and racial distinctions fade away. It is perhaps natural that the home community should resent the rise of the provincials to equality with themselves, and attempt to prevent the attainment of the final dead-level of standardization. In some civilizations the process is completed without undue disturbance of internal tranquillity: in others, on the other hand, fiercely contended civil war has been necessary in order to break the jealously maintained ascendancy of the home community.

The empire of Babylon, which united the many independent cities of the Mesopotamian plain, standardized Mesopotamian culture in an amazing manner, so that in Assyria, in the distant city of Assur, many centuries later, the paramount influence of Babylonian culture cannot be ignored.

The political history of the Roman Empire, from Augustus onward, is very largely a record of the gradual extension of the privilege of citizenship from the Italian peninsula to the outlying provinces. Augustus himself began the degradation of Italy to the provincial level, and Caracalla completed the process two centuries later by the admission of all freeborn inhabitants of the empire to citizenship.

In Islam the same process was not unaccompanied by internal conflict. The Omayyad Caliphs at Damascus upheld the privileges of the Arabian community with a stubborn insistence until overturned by a revolt of the Persians, who set up a new dynasty of Abassid Caliphs at Bagdad.

In the great American democracy of the present day this same process of standardization is very much in evidence, not only to unite the various local centres of colonization, but also to assimilate the immense body of immigration that has poured into the United States. The conflict between the original Anglo-Saxon and immigrant stock for political supremacy is already becoming evident, and centres about the question of 'prohibition' and other Puritan measures imposed by the Anglo-Saxon farming community upon the immigrant urban north-east.

A state of democracy is essentially a state of law. Such an abstract principle as social equality can only be upheld by reference to a system of laws, which is no respecter of persons and dispenses an impartial justice. Indeed, it has been the most striking service of those great leaders, who have founded democracy or have bridled the tyranny of a revolutionary regime, that they have established a code of democratic law that has guaranteed the permanence of democratic institutions for future generations. Democratic Law upholds the social equality of democratic society by a complete negation of all caste distinctions of any kind which are based upon birth and breeding: but its main service to the community lies in its protection of private property against personal or state appropriation. A system of laws may be founded upon any one of a number of ethical principles: that upon which democratic law is based is the common right of the possession and enjoyment of private property, which is extended to the people as a whole. Under autocracy, legal possession and enjoyment of property was almost entirely restricted to the government and its bureaucracy, while such private ownership as was permitted was always open to interference and confiscation by the omnipotent autocrat. In the oligarchic phase, rights of private ownership were extended to the dominant caste and guaranteed to them by a form of law, but measures were introduced to prevent, as far as possible, private ownership on any large scale by the common people. It is only in a state of democracy that the rights of private possession of wealth are extended to the community as a whole. Not only are these rights extended, but democratic law guarantees the continued enjoyment of these rights to every citizen by punishing all offences against the person and property of a citizen and assessing damages for the infringement of property rights by an aggressor. Indeed, the law forms an invisible defence to every citizen, guarding him from dispossession by the unlawful use of force on the part of any third party or organization.

The most powerful and dangerous aggressor who can threaten the citizen in his enjoyment of his rights is the community itself as represented by the government of the state. No single citizen can defy the organized will of his fellow-citizens as expressed by the government, and despite all democratic theory the government of a democratic state can form a grievous tyranny. This is amply shown by the notorious 'revolutionary regime,' which plays its part in the development of nearly every democracy. A real permanently stable state of democracy can only be established when the code of democratic law is placed on a high semi-religious level above the vagaries of political government and out of reach of wilful alteration and suspension. The Law, as a powerful if intangible expression of the democratic spirit of the times, remains a permanent defence for the individual citizen, not only against the individual infringements of his neighbours, but also more usefully against the whole body of his fellow-citizens as represented by the government of the state. Hence in every great democratic empire the Law has been exalted to a position of the highest importance, and in many has enjoyed the added eminence of religious veneration.

In early Mesopotamia the legal code of Hammurabi of Babylon stands out as one of the first endeavours in world history to regulate the relations of the citizens of an empire according to a definite system of laws.

The importance of Roman Law as the basis of the social structure of the Roman Empire need scarcely be stressed, as its effects upon the development of modern European Law can still be traced on all sides.

After the suppression of the Medinians, the Omayyad Caliphs consolidated Islamic Law by reference to the Koran and the recorded sayings of Mahomet. This Moslem code has the same standing in the Near East as Roman Law in Europe.

After the French Revolution, one of the first acts of Napoleon was to codify the gains of the Revolution in the famous 'Code Napoleon,' which has had an inestimable effect upon modern Continental jurisprudence.

In the United States of America, the original framers of American

Law were at such pains to elevate the legal code above the vagaries of political influence that they devised a 'Constitution' of such a remarkable unyielding character that it continually hampers political progress and actual governmental procedure.

The great flood of conquest that marks the success of democratic revolution may pass beyond the former bounds of civilization to subjugate barbarian tribes at a distance; it may even lead to a very considerable extension of the civilized domain, but with the passing of revolutionary activity and the stabilization of democratic empire, conquest comes to an abrupt end and passes rapidly into a state of passive defence against external aggression. It is as if with the advent of the democratic phase civilization loses a certain degree of youthful virility. Peace becomes the ideal of a people that only wish tranquillity to develop to their own best advantage the fruits of civilized co-operation. Conquest is renounced and military activity is restricted to the vigilant defence of the far-flung frontiers of civilization, while all knowledge or experience of military service is gradually forgotten by the inhabitants of the internal provinces of empire.

After the first attempt at the conquest of Syria and Mesopotamia that ended in the disaster of Carchemish, the last democratic Pharaohs of Memphis were content to maintain a vigilant defence at Suez against Mesopotamian aggression.

The Roman Empire reached its greatest permanent Continental extension at the time of Augustus, immediately following the final suppression of the revolutionary regime of the Senate. Later emperors only added Britain as a permanent part of the Roman domain, and built the famous 'limes' of walls and defensive fortifications, which may still be traced across half Europe.

The Moslem Empire of the Caliphate similarly advanced by a rapid series of conquests to a certain maximum extent, after which a period of absolutely stationary defence ensued. Tours marked the utmost advance of the Moslems in the West, while in the East India and the Turkish hordes barred further progress. Henceforth the Caliphate was only too glad to maintain its territories intact against Christian re-conquest from the West and Turkish aggression from the East.

In the modern world, the tendency of democratic empire to 'renounce' war is already becoming evident, and the United States of America has taken the leading part in pressing a peace policy. Having gained the vast North American continent as an object of industrial development, the Americans are only too eager to 'renounce' further conquests.

We have already traced the parallel cultural development of the human individual and of civilization as a superorganism. We have followed our superman from the disciplined 'school' of autocracy through the 'university' of cultural oligarchy to the 'business life' of democracy. We have noted a gradual advance to a peak of cultural attainment in the oligarchic phase similar to that achieved by the average man during his university career, and have traced a further underlying advance to a zenith of material achievement in the maturity of democratic empire similar to the material success of the mature human being in the world of business after leaving the university of pure culture In either case we find that the upward trend of cultural progress has reached, if it has not already passed, its maximum. What can follow?

Up to this point the analogy of the growth and training of the human individual has thrown a most valuable light upon similar problems of growth and training found in the development of the superorganic structure of civilization and it would seem well worth while to trace the analogy further to whatever conclusion, however unexpected it may lead us. The adult human being passes through' no further revolutionary change in social status as marked his passage from school to university life, and from the university to the business world, until he finds himself no longer capable of grappling with the responsibilities and complexities of business and retires into private life. It is this last and concluding revolution in the human career that must now engage our attention, and for which we must seek an analogy in the life-course of civilization. In the last decline of the human individual from maturity to senility before the extinction of death intervenes, a point is reached when the individual is no longer able to withstand the strain of public life, and retires to a comfortable old age protected from the stress of competition in the world of business

This analogy is a particularly difficult one, as exactly as the superorganism cannot 'leave school' when it has passed beyond the 'school age' of autocracy, and is compelled to revolt against and destroy its bureaucratic 'teaching-staff, as again it cannot 'go down' from its oligarchic 'university' and is compelled to suppress its cultured caste of 'dons,' so the superorganism cannot 'retire' from the 'business world' of production, but is compelled to destroy the whole democratic structure of law and order before it can escape from the heavy burden of materialism. Yet the analogy would bid us draw the logical conclusion that civilization as a living, if super, organism must follow the inevitable decline to senility and death, that is the destiny of all life. We must assume that civilization gradually loses its original vitality and relapses by degrees into senile decay, until the very grievous burden of democratic materialism becomes too great to bear. Then as the isolated superman of culture cannot 'retire' from the economic arena, he is compelled to destroy the golden treadmill within which he labours, and stagger away to rest his weary limbs, regardless of the danger that the only rest he may attain may be the everlasting sleep of eternal extinction. Like Samson, he tears down the pillars that support the material edifice of civilization, burying himself beneath the ruins rather than continue to perform the laborious task which maintains the structure.

History has shown time and again how impossible it is for a superorganism to 'retire' from the maintenance of the material structure of democratic empire, without finding immediate extinction in a flood of barbarian invasion. The world of supermen, less humane than the world of human existence, has its barbarian wolves who tear down the ageing civilizations when they become too weary to carry and wield their weapons of defence. There has been no mercy for the senile on the higher plane of superorganic existence in the past. The question of the old age of modern civilizations, now that the peril of external barbarism is practically extinguished, is one of the most interesting problems of superorganic speculation. A 'comfortable' old age of socialism, if still of doubtful practicability, is at least a remote possibility in the future of modern civilizations.

Turning from the analogy to historical record, we find that the liberty of the individual under democratic law to amass unlimited personal wealth at the expense of his weaker and less efficient brethren leads to a rapid subversion of the original idealist equality of democratic society. Within a few generations the division of society into rich and poor becomes a much more grievous inequality, and one much harder to bear, than the former caste divisions of oligarchy. Equality of opportunity is not sufficient to produce a true equality in society, as the natural differences of personal efficiency and industry give the strong an inevitable advantage over the weak. The very stability of democratic law and order, like the tranquillity of a mountain lake after the turmoil of a descending torrent, merely encourages the buoyant objects suspended in its waters to rise to the surface, while the heavier proletarian element sinks to form the mud of the depths. As long as this stability is maintained like the tranquillity of the lake, nothing can rectify the division of society into rich and poor; plutocrat scum remains plutocrat scum, while proletarian mud remains proletarian mud. This is obviously the case when we remember that the right of inheritance is upheld by democratic law, and hence wealth breeds wealth, while poverty cannot breed ought else but poverty.[15] Jesus, who was born into a dawning age of democracy, remarked with great insight, 'To him that hath shall be given, and from him that hath not shall be taken even that which he hath.'

Even in the early code of democratic law promulgated by Hammurabi of Babylon the division of society into rich and poor is clearly reflected.

In the Roman Empire the accumulation of wealth by the rich took the agricultural form of the dispossession of small-holding farmers and the formation of vast plantations. The former peasantry was reduced to a destitute proletariat, which tended to gravitate into the large cities, where free bread and entertainment might be obtained. The Law and Order of the pax romana enabled plutocracy to reach an unbearable logical conclusion of economic inequality.

It is impossible to read the Arabian Nights, which give such a living picture of life in the Caliphate, without being struck with the importance of money and wealth as the basis of the Islamic society of the time.

In the modern world, the United States alone look back upon a considerable period of democratic empire, and it is in the United States that plutocracy is already in the process of development. The holy rights of property, nowhere so fanatically upheld as in America, have produced with logical inevitability the millionaires and omnipotent trusts which dominate American life today.

Democratic materialism which encourages the self-indulgence of the people as individuals brings an inevitable degeneration in its train. The democratic individual is no longer willing to sacrifice himself or his interests to civilization as a super-organic entity greater than himself; on the contrary, he expects civilization to serve him in complete contradiction to the upward trend of the metaphysical scheme to a higher integration of human service. The democratic citizen is no longer prepared to devote his whole life for small reward to the advancement of the civilization within which he lives; on the contrary, he plunges into the 'men's' world of business to grasp the largest possible share of the material fruits of this civilization for his own enjoyment. Even the simple primitive ideal of patriotism ceases to move men's hearts,

---

15   Modern states seek to restrict inheritance by 'death duties,' but this is only a palliation, and it is difficult to prevent avoidance by various means.

and the citizen, while enjoying all the advantages that civilization renders, forgets the duty of service and defence which civilization must claim in return. Most serious of all, the individual deliberately shirks the responsibility of begetting and rearing a large family, owing to the inevitable sacrifice of his or her personal interests to those of the children. As a climax of self-seeking individualism, democracy actually denies civilization the very life-blood of human beings, without which it is no more than a mass of unmeaning masonry.

Our knowledge of ancient civilizations is not in general sufficiently intimate for us to trace such intangible effects as those of individual degeneration, but at least we do find a decline of patriotic service in the defence of the state in the last stages of every democratic era.

In the Roman Empire, however, we find definite record of progressive degeneration, which was most strikingly illustrated by the decline of the birth-rate, which led to the actual depopulation of whole provinces.

In the modern world, democracy has scarcely been long enough established for degenerative effects to have become evident, but already the decline of the birth-rate in all democratic states is very noticeable. In America there are a number of medical authorities who are convinced that the increasing dependence of American society upon mechanical transport and extravagant steam heating, etc., cannot fail to have a general adverse effect upon the physical well-being of the race.

The inability of the degenerate, self-indulgent citizens of later democratic empire to undertake their own defence against the ever present threat of barbarian invasion, or the pressure of a younger and more virile civilization, presents a difficult military problem to the imperial government. The solution almost invariably arrived at is to employ mercenaries enlisted either from among the barbarians themselves or from among the subjects of another more virile civilization. The great wealth of plutocracy enables this vicarious form of defence to be undertaken, but the most obvious dangers arise on account of the racial kinship between the mercenaries and the very enemies against which they are to be employed. As long as sufficient funds are forthcoming to pay even exorbitant rates of pay to the mercenary troops a certain stability of military defence may be maintained, but the burden of such an expensive defensive system weighs more and more heavily upon waning democracy until inevitably the breaking-point is reached.

Civilization As Divine Superman

In the last period of independent Egyptian democracy, under the XXVI dynasty, the entire defence of Suez against the Persians was delegated to Greek mercenaries.

In the later Roman Empire, similarly, barbarian Goths were engaged as a mercenary defence force.

Both the Caliphate and the Tang-Sung Empire in China employed Turks from Central Asia.

In the modern world this terrible question of the employment of barbarian mercenaries in the form of a defence force or a police service has happily not yet arisen. Only France has adopted the enlistment of barbarian African troops in her territorial army. H. G. Wells, in his Sleeper Awakes, has, however, pointed out the future possibility of the employment of African negroes as a police force to suppress disaffected revolt among a degenerate proletariat.

The first violation of the frontiers of civilization by the external barbarians comes as a terrible shock to democracy. The gradual degeneration of the fighting spirit of the people of the democratic era passes unnoticed by themselves, especially as they are rendered particularly self-confident by the evident material triumphs of their civilization, and the sudden realization that the defence of the whole material fabric of civilization is threatened awakens democracy to the need of a supreme effort. It is perhaps the plutocratic element alone that is really supremely interested in the continued existence of civilization, but the plutocracy represents the wealth and power of civilization, and is best fitted to undertake such measures as are necessary to continue its existence in the face of barbarian aggression. The plutocratic owners of wealth throughout democratic civilization voluntarily submit themselves to the most efficient military leadership available, and place their entire financial resources at the disposal of the mercenary armies, in the hope of averting the very evident danger of the entire collapse of that democratic system of law and order upon which their plutocratic ascendancy depends. Civilization is handed over unconditionally to military dictatorship, and the last stage of democracy is, strange to say, a pure 'militarism' even more drastic than under autocracy.

After the first Persian conquest of Egypt the Egyptian people actually succeeded by a violent effort in ejecting the Persians, when several dynasties of military Pharaohs maintained Egyptian independence for a further sixty years.

The Political Cycle

In the Roman Empire the crisis of barbarian invasion in the third century was a tremendous shock to Roman tranquillity, and was the direct cause of the militarist regime of the 'Dominate,' which held sway for the remaining period of imperial unity.

It was the internal revolt of Negro slaves, Khorrami communists, and Karmathian puritans that threatened the Caliphate and brought about the regime of the Turkish generals, who usurped temporal power from the Caliphs.

In China, the Sung dynasty formed a similar military regime after the collapse of the Tang, but soon relapsed into the last humiliating resort of direct tribute payment to the barbarian hordes in return for freedom from devastating raids.

By the time that democratic law and order have given rise to plutocracy, civilization as a superorganic spirit has practically ceased to exist, stifled under the load of materialism. The majority of the people, reduced to a dispossessed proletariat, weighed down by the accumulated wealth of the plutocratic few and the burden of militarism, are weary of civilization and would welcome its complete extinction. The spiritual reality of human support being withdrawn, all that remains of civilization is the actual material wealth, which forms a golden shell about its degenerate human contents. The plutocracy contrives to survive for a time, in face of its repudiation by the civilized subjects of the state, by purchasing support by means of its immense wealth from the surrounding barbarian hordes. The rich introduce barbarians into the army and police force of civilization to replace the disaffected proletarian element, upon whose loyalty and virility they can no longer depend. As the declining birth-rate deprives civilization of a sufficiency of subject-peoples, barbarians are deliberately settled in numbers within the bounds of civilization. Thus for a time the mere existence of the accumulated wealth of plutocracy enables a synthetic imitation of civilization to be maintained, long after the real superorganism has succumbed, by an incongruous association of extreme material sophistication and barbarian simplicity.

Obviously such an attempt on the part of plutocracy to perpetuate the mere material structure of civilization with purchased barbarian assistance is doomed to early failure. It is as if a man shipwrecked on a cannibal island were to purchase his life from the cannibals by daily tribute from the stores he had saved from the wreck. After his ammunition was exhausted he might engage some of the natives to act as a mercenary bodyguard against the remainder, but his survival would depend purely upon his personal prestige, and a chance accident might at any moment bring the end, while the decline of his stores would in any case place a definite limit upon the duration of the farce. Plutocracy also survives in face of its complete dependence upon barbarian toleration only by means of the accumulated prestige of civilization, and may at any moment be extinguished by some chance military incident. The inevitable decline of plutocratic wealth itself brings ever nearer the final crisis, when the tribute demanded by the barbarians can no longer be rendered.

When the point is reached that the plutocratic wreck of civilization can no longer produce sufficient material contributions to satisfy barbarian extortion, or should before that time the barbarians become aware of their power, then plutocracy is overwhelmed in a flood of barbarian invasion which destroys the remnant of material wealth and prosperity in an orgy of loot and rapine. The nomad peoples of the open steppes and plains migrate in whole nations with their flocks and herds across the borders of civilization and pour in a stream of despoiling hordes through the countryside from city to city. Primitive society can at last come into its own once more, can take its revenge upon the unnatural superorganic growth of civilization which has arisen in its midst. The nomads alone, however, are not sufficiently numerous to account for the huge multitudes that follow barbarian leadership. The fact is that the first barbarian forces which turn against plutocracy are immediately joined by immense numbers of liberated slaves and other members of the degraded proletariat, who are only too eager to join in the spoliation of the material wealth of civilization and the persecution of those members of plutocratic society who have been their hard taskmasters. It is no doubt to this slave element that the terrible atrocities and 'vandalism' of barbarian invasion are to be attributed, as while the barbarians are only in search of the spoil and booty of the cities, the liberated slaves have a private account of their own to settle with the rich owners of these cities.

Within the period of history three separate barbarian invasions of decadent democracy are known.

Shortly after 2000 A.D. a practically simultaneous nomad invasion from Central Asia destroyed both the Babylonian and Early Egyptian civilizations. In Egypt the Hyksos or 'Shepherd Kings' ravaged the country with fire and sword, while in Babylonia the Kassites slowly submerged and degraded the highly sophisticated civilization of Babylon. The invasion and destruction of the Roman Empire by the Goths and Vandals is the classical example of cultural eclipse.

The thirteenth and fourteenth centuries A.D. saw the last and greatest nomad scourge, when the Mongols attacked and overthrew the Sung Empire in China, the Caliphate in Mesopotamia, and the Moslem Empire of Delhi in India, one after the other. This terrible, almost world-wide nomad flood actually washed up against Eastern Europe, conquering Russia, Poland, Hungary, and Silesia before it ebbed once more into Central Asia.

4. THE ANARCHIC PHASE

When barbarian invasion overwhelms civilization, the conditions of primitive society are re-established for a time over the region formerly the seat of cultural co-operation. Primitive individual equality takes the place of the specialization and differentiation peculiar to civilization. In fact, the deceptive equality of opportunity in democracy, that gave rise to the contradictory inequality of plutocracy, is replaced, as demanded by the communist anarchists, by the real equality of wealth and income peculiar to primitive tribal institutions. Unfortunately, this new equality is only to be attained at the expense of the complete collapse of the economic structure of civilization, and is rather an equality of destitution than one of wealth.

Society relapses, when the loot of plutocratic civilization is exhausted, to primitive nomadism or agriculture, and the surviving remnant of the mixed barbarian and slave population finds a means of livelihood in tending flocks and herds or engaging in primitive methods of tilling the soil. The superorganism has been destroyed and Nature returns into her own. The nomads and agriculturists recognize practically no differentiation of office in the herdsman and agriculturist occupations, and each individual is expected to show his ability in the common task of all. In the early tradition of almost every people of an inter-cultural barbarism, a form of tribal communism, such as that of the Anglo-Saxons in England, may be traced. Much of the land and many of the animals are held in common by the local community, and a very great deal of communal labour is undertaken by the individual. Indeed, in the first beginnings of these primitive tribes communal ownership of land and livestock, and communal pooling of labour resources, would seem to have been the rule. Thus the communism of declining civilization may well be an unconscious reaction from the burden of civilization to the equality and common ownership of primitive tribal life before the advent of cultural differentiation: the psychological 'infantilism' of the social 'psyche.'

Civilization As Divine Superman

The destruction wrought by barbarian invasion of civilization in conjunction with the anarchic revolt of the internal disaffected proletariat is in every case terrible. Great cities are reduced to uninhabited ruins, even local towns are deserted, while country villas, as the luxurious abodes of the hated plutocracy, are burned to the ground. All the great material triumphs of past culture are lost and destroyed. Roads, aqueducts, baths, and circuses crumble to ruins in disuse and neglect. Civilization being already extinct in spirit, its material outward form also returns to dust and ashes.

But the destruction may exceed by far the demolition of the material structure of plutocracy. The barbarians who take the leading part in the conquest of the civilized domain are nomadic tribesmen from the steppes and plains of the north, and are not only antagonistic to civilization, but even more so to the primitive form of agriculture from which civilization has arisen. Hence the triumph of nomadism has the even more disastrous result of degrading much of the conquered territory formerly devoted to agriculture and its attendant civilization to mere pasture lands for the flocks and herds of primitive nomad tribes. It may even follow, under the burning tropical sun, that the neglect of irrigation by nomad barbarians reduces prosperous regions to such desert aridity that they will not even support the flocks and herds for whose pasturage they have been degraded.

The loot, rapine, and wanton destruction wrought by the barbarians who conquered the Roman Empire have made the names 'Goth' and 'Vandal' synonymous with hatred and persecution of art and culture to the present day. In an incredibly short space of time all the material wealth and splendour that was Rome was demolished and humbled to the dust.

The Mongols, as confirmed nomads from the Central Asian steppes, completed their destruction of civilization by the almost total eradication of agriculture as well in those regions where their devastating hordes had passed. The Caliphate, as the object of their earliest and most deadly attacks, suffered most severely under this primitive ferocity, and there are large areas in the former domain of Moslem Empire which have been reduced to this day to arid and forbidding wastes. It is indeed difficult to credit sandy Mesopotamia and desert Central Asia with the flourishing prosperity that was theirs a thousand years ago.

As long as civilization survives, and especially during the last defensive epoch, there is a sharp dividing line between what is within and without the borders of civilization. Civilized peoples are apt to regard their own particular world region as the whole world, and to disregard all regions external to it. In old times this attitude took the form of a geographical misconception, which placed the centre of the world within the civilized domain with a surrounding waste inhabited by barbarians. We have only to examine a map of the world drawn in classical or even medieval times in Europe to appreciate this fact, for in these maps the Mediterranean is in truth the 'Internal Sea' about which the rest of the world is centred. Even within the last few centuries the Jesuit geographer, Ricci, when constructing a map of the world at the command of the Chinese emperor during the seventeenth century, was compelled to choose a form of projection that made allowance for Chinese prejudices by making the 'Empire of the Middle' appear as the centre of the world surrounded by a foreshortened region inhabited by 'outer barbarians.'

When barbarians invaded the domain of civilization the sharp boundary between civilization and external barbarism is swept away for a time and a more complete realization of geographical reality is granted to the survivors of civilization. They appreciate at last how small is the world region to which their former culture was confined, and how vast the external world and the forces at work within it. They become for the first time cognizant of distant civilizations far across the seas of nomad barbarism. Intercultural relations are suddenly opened with distant regions, and the remnants of culture partake for a time in the fellowship of nomad existence, which knows no boundaries on the open steppes, and extends unbroken from continent to continent, between civilization and civilization. Anarchy and barbarism are truly international, knowing no concentration for the purpose of cultural co-operation.

In early Egypt the temporary incorporation of Egypt into the international barbarian sphere is illustrated by the extraordinary dispersion of the scarabs and other relics of the Hyksos kings to Syria, and even Mesopotamia and Crete. In fact, no other Egyptian kings enjoy such apparent widespread recognition.

The Teutonic peoples that poured into the Roman Empire from the north opened the eyes of the Mediterranean nations to the existence of Northern Europe, and the Moslem pressure from the south in the succeeding centuries directed the dawning energies of the new European civilization towards this promising region as the seat of reviving culture.

Civilization As Divine Superman

The appalling Mongol scourge which destroyed three Asiatic civilizations, one after the other, had one very valuable intercultural effect, when it brought the several seats of civilization in the Old World for the first time into direct contact with one another. At one time the Mongol sway reached from Poland to Manchuria, and from Siberia to the borders of Egypt and India. European travellers, like Marco Polo, venturing among the barbarians on the borders of Poland or from the shores of the Mediterranean in Syria, might proceed, unimpeded by national boundaries, through Central Asia to the distant realms of India or China. Thus for a brief period international boundaries were broken down, and Europe began to realize the presence of distant people of great native culture far away at the other ends of the world, before the barbarians were eventually repulsed and the distant civilizations vanished once more behind the isolation of their frontier defences.

The huge migrations and disturbances attendant upon the collapse of civilization lead to a complete change in the relationships of national and racial groups. The tremendous vortex caused by the submergence of the super-organic ship of state in the sea of barbarism swirls the surrounding barbarian peoples into the void, and mixes them together into a new solution in which floats the wreckage of civilization. Not only are the many racial groups of the surrounding barbarians merged into a new people, but the degenerate remnant of civilized peoples mingles with the virile barbarians to form a new conglomerate social organization. In this latter process the extreme contempt felt by the true barbarian towards the miserable slaves of former plutocratic civilization counteracts the tendency to combination, and the distinction between the barbarian and slave element may well be pronounced until a much later date, when the revival of culture has already progressed to a high level. However, the general result of barbarian invasion and conquest is the introduction of a new virile stock of barbarian origin into the world region that was formerly the seat of a declining cultural system, to replace the degeneration and depopulation that has depleted the civilized community. This new stock intermingles with the old, and forms a new and more vigorous subject of superorganic reorganization.

In order to have a clear impression of the cyclic nature of the life-course of civilization, a diagram illustrating the political cycle is given here. As cyclic motion is best represented in a circular form, the diagram has been formed of four quadrants, A, B, C, and D, each of which is equivalent to one of the sections of this chapter.

THE POLITICAL CYCLE

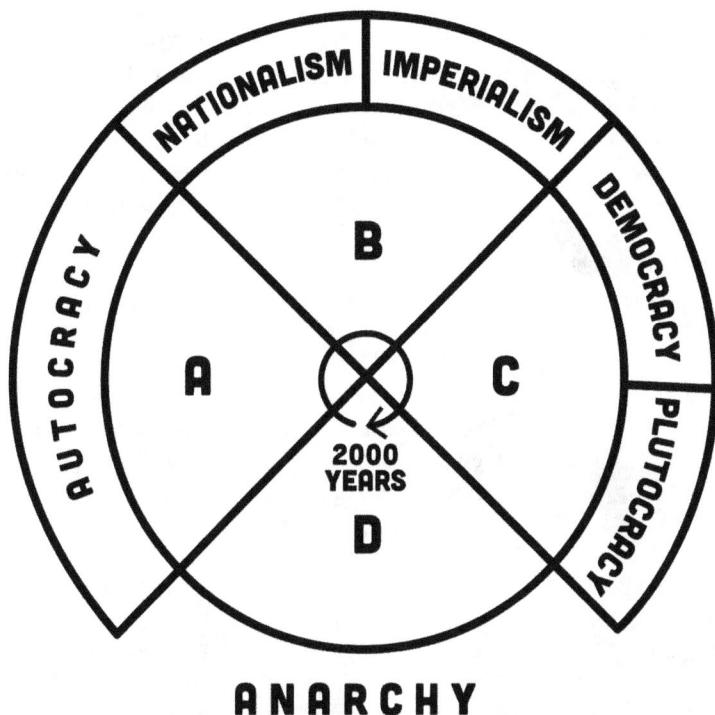

ANARCHY

This is the typical ground or basic cycle of civilization. It has an undoubted 'nadir' in quadrant D, but it is less easy to agree upon its 'zenith.' The Catholic Church would favour quadrant A: our empire builders quadrant B: while America is quite convinced that quadrant C is excellent and leading rapidly to a millennium.

Quadrant B has been divided between Nationalism and Imperialism in, equal parts, but this division is quite arbitrary. In some cases either one or the other phase entirely fails to materialize, or the division in time between the two phases may be quite other than equal. In quadrant C, on the other hand, the development of Plutocracy out of Democracy is an inevitable process.

The actual lines of cleavage between the several phases of this cycle indicate periods of intense disturbance accompanied by warfare internal or external; but the phases themselves, with the exception of the unstable Nationalist epoch, are periods of tranquillity and comparative peace.

Civilization As Divine Superman

CIVILIZATION	AUTOCRATIC EMPIRE	NATIONAL DISRUPTION
4000 - 1700 B.C. EARLY EGYPTIAN Original.	4000 - 2500 B.C. OLD KINGDOM AT MEMPHIS The great autocratic pyramid builders.	2500 - 2000 B.C. LOCAL FEUDAL AUTONOMY Independence of Heracleopolis, Thebes, Elephantine, etc.
1500 - 300 B.C. LATE EGYPTIAN Descendant.	1500 - 1100 B.C. NEW KINGDOM AT THEBES Theban princes expel Hykos and establish centralised autocratic empire conquering Nubian and Syria	1100 - 750 B.C. LOCAL AUTONOMY Local generals and governors make themselves independent of declining Thebian authority.
1100 - 150 B.C. PHOENICIAN Divergent.	(see Late Egyptian Civilisation.)	1100 - 350 B.C. SYRIAN STATES Independence of Syrian cities following withdrawal of Egyptians. Maritime made of Tyre and Sidon.
2500 B.C. - 400 A.D. MEDITERRANEAN Offshoot.	2500 - 1400 B.C. MINOAN EMPIRE Powerful maritime autocracy centered upon palatial Cnossus.	1400 - 350 B.C. MYCENEAN AND GREEK CITY STATES Independent cities engaged in mutual rivalry and conflict.
1050 A.D. - present EUROPEAN Descendant	1050 - 1550 A.D. THE PAPACY Autocratic church government, building great abbeys and cathedrals and organising crusades as wars of conquest.	1550 A.D. - present NATIONAL STATES Following the Reformation, many national states are formed, which engage in internecine warfare.

The Political Cycle

IMPERIALISM	DEMOCRATIC EMPIRE	BARBARIAN INVASION
(Attempted hegemony by Heracleopolis failed.)	2000 - 1700 B.C. MIDDLE KINGDOM AT THEBES Benevolent Pharaohs improve irrigation system of Nile.	1700 B.C. HYKOSOS Sudden invasion and destruction by shepherds.
750 - 650 B.C. ETHIOPIANS Negroid peoples from Nubia conquer Egypt and establish a racial oligarchy.	650 - 300 B.C. RENAISSANCE AT MEMPHIS An invasion of Assyrians drives out the Ethiopians, and benevolent Pharaohs rule at Memphis.	300 B.C. PERSIANS AND GREEKS Repeated Persian invasion culminates in the conquest of Alexander.
350 - 150 B.C. CARTHAGE Phoenician colonies in North Africa for a new imperial domain overseas after the fall of Tyre.	(Jewish influences in European civilisation linger to the present.)	
350 - 150 B.C. MACEDONIA Conquest of Greek city states by Philip of Macedon. Great Empire of his son Alexander.	150 B.C. - 400 A.D. ROMAN EMPIRE Democratic Rome conquers Carthage and Macedonia in turn, founding a great benevolent empire.	400 A.D. GOTHS AND VANDALS Repeated barbarian invasion gradually overwhelms Rome.
(Pan-Europa.) (Attempted hegemony by Germany failed.)	(The United States of Europe. Still a dream of the future.)	

CIVILIZATION	AUTOCRATIC EMPIRE	NATIONAL DISRUPTION
1500 A.D. - present LATIN AMERICAN	1500 - 1800 A.D. PAPAL AND CROWN CONTROL Conquest and settlement under the inspiration of papal crusades. Jesuit missions in Paraguay and California.	1800 A.D. - present REPUBLICAN STATES Revolt against European control. Local independence and national rivalry between states.
Divergent.		
1650 A.D. - present NORTH AMERICAN Divergent.	(See European Civilization.)	(See European Civilization.)
1750 A.D. - present OCEANIC Divergent.	(See European Civilization.)	(See European Civilization.)
3800 - 1800 B.C. BABYLONIAN Descendant from Sumerian.	3800 - 3300 B.C. EMPIRE OF AKKAD Autocratic military state founded by Sargon, who rules from Persian Gulf to Mediterranean.	3300-2600 B.C. LOCAL AUTONOMY Independence of local cities under the suzerainty of Ur.
1500 - 1100 B.C. HITTITE Descendant-Offshoot.	1500 - 1100 B.C. HITTITE EMPIRE Founded in Eastern Asia by Subbiluliuma.	(Destroyed by rise of Assyria.)
1100 B.C. - 1250 A.D. MESTOPOTAMIAN Descendant	1100 - 300 B.C. ASSYRIA AND PERSIA Military autocracy founded by the Assyrians and adopted by the invading Persians.	(Not developed.)

The Political Cycle

IMPERIALISM	DEMOCRATIC EMPIRE	BARBARIAN INVASION
(Not developed.) 1750 A.D. - present BRITISH EMPIRE The command of the seas has enabled the British to conquer and colonize a great Empire overseas.	1650 A.D. - present UNITED STATES OF AMERICA. Democratic empire founded by refugees from English Revolution.	(Signs of degeneration and social disintegration already appearing.)
2600 - 2350 B.C. THE ELAMITES The Elamites from the hills of Persia conquer Mesopotamia and establish a racial oligarchy.	2350 - 1800 B.C. BABYLON Hammurabi of Babylon expels the Elamites and founds democratic empire with code of laws.	1800 B.C. THE KASSITES A further Semetic barbarian invasion submerges Babylon.
300 B.C. - 650 A.D. HELLENISM Conquest of Persia by Greeks under Alexander, who form a racial oligarchy. Parthians adopt similar social organization later.	650 - 1250 A.D. THE CALIPHATE Mahomet founds Islam and Moslem armies conquer immense empire. Democratic Law and benevolent government.	1250 A.D. MONGOLS Turks, followed by Mongols, invade and destroy Caliphate.

The Political Cycle

CIVILISATION	AUTOCRATIC EMPIRE	NATIONAL DISRUPTION
800 - 1500 A.D. ZANZIBAR Divergent.	(See Mesopotamian Civilization.)	
1450 A.D. - present LEVANTINE Descendant.	1450 - 1900 A.D. THE SULTANATE Powerful military autocracy captures Constantinople and conquers Eastern Europe.	1900 A.D. - present DICTATORSHIP Remnants of Turkish Empire from autonomous states under local dictators.
300 B.C. - 1400 A.D. ARYAN Descendant from Sudra.	300 B.C. - 250 A.D. BUDDHIST EMPIRES Military autocracy founded by Chandragupta and developed by Asoka, who adopts the Buddhist faith.	250 - 1050 A.D. RAJA STATES With the decline of Buddhism, local rulers or 'Rajas' become independent.
200 B.C. - 1600 A.D. SINHALESE Divergent.	200 B.C. - 1200 A.D. MAHINDA EMPIRE Autocratic hierachy founded by son of Asoka, when Aryans invade Ceylon.	1200 - 1600 A.D. SEVEN KINGSDOMS Autocratic empire eventually gives way to disruption.
100 - 1500 A.D. JAVANESE Offshoot.	100 - 600 A.D. BUDDHIST EMPIRE OF JAVA Inspired by Buddhist missionaries from India.	600 - 1400 A.D. LOCAL AUTONOMY Independent kingdoms on various Malayan Islands.
100 A.D. - present INDO-CHINESE Offshoot.	100 - 1300 A.D. BURMESE EMPIRE Powerful autocratic empire centered upon the capital city of Pagan, which is finally destroyed by the Mongols.	1300 A.D. - present NATIONAL STATES After the fall of Pagan Siam, Pegu, Cambodia, etc., become fully independent.

Civilization As Divine Superman

IMPERIALISM	DEMOCRATIC EMPIRE	BARBARIAN INVASION
(See Mestopotamian Civilization.)	800 - 1500 A.D. ZANZIBAR EMPIRE	(Destroyed by Portuguese.)
	Political refugees from Bagdad found colonial empire on coast of East Africa.	
(Attempted hegemony by Cholu 'Rajaraja' failed.)	1050 - 1400 A.D. EMPIRE OF DELHI Moslems from Afghanistan conquer India, establishing empire with capital Delhi.	1400 A.D. MONGOLS Timur takes and sacks Delhi.
(Destroyed by Dutch.)		
(Not developed.)	1400 - 1500 A.D. MOSLEM EMPIRE Islam reaches East Indies.	(Destroyed by Portuguese.)
(Attempted hegemony by Siam failed; other states were, however conquered by Europeans.)		

CIVILIZATION	AUTOCRATIC EMPIRE	NATIONAL DISRUPTION
1550 A.D. - present INDIAN Descendant.	1550 - 1750 A.D. MONGOL EMPIRE Great military autocracy founded by descendants of the original Mongol conquerors of Delhi.	1750 - 1800 A.D. MAHRATTA STATES Revolt of Hindu principalities from Mongul authority.
1800 B.C. - 1250 A.D. EARLY CHINESE Original.	1800 - 800 B.C. SHANG AND CHOU EMPIRES. Centralized autocracies with "mandarin" bureaucracy.	800 - 200 B.C. THE CONTENDING STATES With the decline of Chou authority many independent states arise, which engage in warfare.
1350 A.D. - present LATE CHINESE Descendant.	1350 - 1600 A.D. MING EMPIRE Autocratic empire at Pekin following the expulsion of the Mongols.	1600 - 1650 A.D. Disruption. Revolt of 'robber' bands, which seriously threatens the empire.
400 A.D. - present JAPANESE Offshoot.	400 - 1150 A.D. MIKADOS AND FUJIWARA SHOGUNS. Autocratic empire centered upon Kioto, ruled at first by the Mikados, and later by their Shogun regents.	1150 - 1600 A.D. DAIMYOS Upon the decline of the Fujiwara Shoguns, Japan splits up into many Daimyo principalities.
100 (?) - 1500 A.D. CENTRAL AMERICAN Descendant (?).	100 - 600 A.D. (?) TOLTEC EMPIRE Founded by the legendary autocrat Quetzalcoatl.	600 - 1500 A.D. MAYA CITY STATES These cities still flourished in Yucatan at the time of the Spanish Invasion.
1200 (?) - 1500 A.D. PERUVIAN Original.	1200 - 1500 A.D. INCA EMPIRE Founded by the legendary Manco Capec, this great military autocracy extends its sway far up and down the coast of South America.	(Destroyed by the Spaniards.)

Civilization As Divine Superman

IMPERIALISM	DEMOCRATIC EMPIRE	BARBARIAN INVASION
1800 A.D. - present BRITISH RAJ British conquer Mahratta and Nabob principalities, establishing a racial oligarchy.	(Swaraj.) (Unrealized object of present Indian ambitions.)	
200 B.C. - 600 A.D. HAN EMPIRE Ts'in conquers other Chinese states to establish a united Empire.	600 - 1250 A.D. TAND AND SUNG EMPIRE Yuan Kien proclaims new code of laws and establishes a democratic administration.	1250 A.D. MONGOLS Invade and conquer China.
1650 - 1900 A.D. THE MANCHUS Take advantage of internal disorder to conquer China.	1900 A.D. - present CHINESE REPUBLIC Cantonese revolt against Manchus to establish a democratic republic.	
1600 - 1850 A.D. TOKUGAWA SHOGUNATE Three great statesmen reunite Japan under the oligarchic sway of the Samurai caste.	1850 A.D. - present WESTERNIZED JAPAN A revolution deposes the Samurai and restores the personal authority of the Mikado.	
(Aztec attempt to gain hegemony interrupted by Spanish conquest.)		

Civilization As Divine Superman

We are now in a position to discuss the duration of the various phases of the cultural cycle and the average length of life of civilization as a superorganism.

Taking the autocratic phase alone, we can best judge its average duration from descendant civilizations, as in original and offshoot cultural systems the origin of culture is inevitably wrapped in the mystery of legend, and accurate chronological data is lacking.

BABYLONIAN CIVILIZATION		
Empire of Akkad	3800 - 3300 B.C.	500 years
MESOPOTAMIAN CIVILIZATION		
Assyria and Persia	1100 - 300 B.C.	800 years
LEVANTINE CIVILIZATION		
The Sultanate	1450 - 1900 A.D.	450 years
LATE EGYPTIAN CIVILIZATION		
The New Kingdom	1500 - 1100 B.C.	400 years
EUROPEAN CIVILIZATION		
The Papacy	1050 - 1550 A.D.	500 years
ARYAN CIVILIZATION		
Buddhist Empires	300 B.C. - 250 A.D.	550 years
INDIAN CIVILIZATION		
The Mogul Empire	1550 - 1750 A.D.	200 years
LATE CHINESE CIVILIZATION		
Ming Empire	1350 - 1600 A.D.	250 years
	Average	450 years

The whole period of oligarchic rule must be taken as one, owing to the fact that in some civilizations either one or other of the nationalist and imperialist phases has not been developed.

Actually, these two forms of oligarchic regime are complementary, and if the attainment of a hegemony be too long delayed, democratic revolution will intervene in the midst of a typical national disruption.

The Political Cycle

EARLY EGYPTIAN CIVILIZATION Local Feudal Autonomy	2500-2000 B.C.	500 years
LATE EGYPTIAN CIVILIZATION Oligarchic Phase	1100- 650 B.C.	450 years
PHOENICIAN CIVILIZATION Oligarchic Phase	1100- 150 B.C.	950 years
MEDITERRANEAN CIVILIZATION Mycenaeans and Greeks	1400- 150 B.C.	1,250 years
BABYLONIAN CIVILIZATION Oligarchic Phase	3300-2350 B.C.	950 years
MESOPOTAMIAN CIVILIZATION Neo-Hellenism	300 B.C.- 650A.D.	950 years
ARYAN CIVILIZATION Raja States	250-1050 A.D.	800 years
EARLY CHINESE CIVILIZATION Oligarchic Phase	800 B.C.-600 A.D.	1,400 years
LATE CHINESE CIVILIZATION Oligarchic Phase	1600-1900 A.D.	300 years
JAPANESE CIVILIZATION Oligarchic Phase	1150-1850 A.D.	700 years
	Average	800 years

The duration of such democratic phases as have reached their conclusion in the extinction of civilization is as follows:

EARLY EGYPTIAN CIVILIZATION Middle Kingdom	2000-1700 B.C.	300 years
LATE EGYPTIAN CIVILIZATION Renaissance at Memphis	650- 300 B.C.	350 years
MEDITERRANEAN CIVILIZATION Roman Empire	150 B.C.- 400 A.D.	550 years

BABYLONIAN CIVILIZATION Babylon	2350-1800 B.C.	550 years
MESOPOTAMIAN CIVILIZATION The Caliphate	650-1250 A.D.	600 years
ZANZIBAR CIVILIZATION Zanzibar Empire	800-1500 A.D.	700 years
ARYAN CIVILIZATION Empire of Delhi Early	1050-1400 A.D.	350 years
CHINESE CIVILIZATION Tang and Sung Empire	600-1250 A.D.	650 years
	Average	500 years

It would appear from an addition of the duration of these several phases that the total life-course of a civilization is on the average 1,750 years.

The duration of the intercultural period of barbarism is also of interest.

BABYLONIAN TO HITTITE Kassite barbarism	1800-1500 B.C.	300 years
EARLY TO LATE EGYPTIAN Hyksos barbarism	1700-1500 B.C.	200 years
MEDITERRANEAN TO EUROPEAN Teutonic barbarism	400-1050 A.D.	650 years
EARLY TO LATE CHINESE Mongol barbarism	1250-1350 A.D.	100 years
MESOPOTAMIAN TO LEVANTINE Mongol barbarism	1250-1450 A.D.	200 years
ARYAN TO INDIAN Mongol barbarism	1400-1550 A.D.	150 years
	Average	250 years

We have therefore a total average duration of the entire cultural cycle from one phase of an original civilization to a similar phase of its descendant of 2,000 years.

By a strict chronological application of this period we should arrive at the conclusion that Europe is in somewhat the condition of the Mediterranean at 100 B.C., which is not at all a bad analogy, while we arrive at the similar conclusion that the Westernizing of the Near East is a repetition of the Hellenization of Mesopotamia at about the same epoch.

Actually we cannot apply this period as a fixed measure of superorganic development any more than we can apply the measure of age to human beings without consideration of their individuality. Some civilizations, like those of China and the Mediterranean, have exceeded two thousand five hundred years of life, while others, like Late Egyptian civilization, have been stunted and finally extinguished by foreign intervention within scarcely more than a thousand years. Still, we may accept approximately two thousand years as the average duration of the cultural cycle, when all due allowance is made for the individual development of each civilization as a separate superorganism.

Chapter 4

The Economic Cycle

Barbarism differs most materially from civilization in the economic sphere. It is the ability of agriculture to accumulate capital in the form of grain that enables civilization to arise from the cultivation of the soil. Pastoral and hunting communities are debarred from any large accumulation of available capital by their dependence upon animal life, and hence cannot form that economic reserve from which civilization is financed. Civilization is the product of the surplus energies of a community after their primitive needs and requirements have been satisfied, and hence in the economic sphere capital as the surplus of production over expenditure is the essential basis of civilization. The primitive agricultural community produces for the first time a large surplus of food over and above the needs of the cultivators, and this great surplus is at the disposal of dawning civilization, to nourish the new superorganism. The peasantry remain always with us as the primitive source from which civilization has sprung. The self-sacrifice of this semi-barbaric community alone has enabled civilization to exist, and it only continues to exist at their pleasure. Within recent years, when political disorder and debased paper money have destroyed the confidence of the peasantry in Central and Eastern Europe, we have seen how their refusal to produce the usual surplus of food, which we take so much for granted, has brought civilization tottering almost to its fall. In Russia, particularly, the early failure of the Soviet regime to come to terms with the peasantry almost starved civilization out of existence.

It is well to remember this dual economic structure of society: civilization subsisting as a higher parasitic organism upon the surplus production of a primitive agricultural community. The perennial conflict of city and country, sophisticated townsman and ignorant yokel, has, as have so many common passions, a real significance as the conflict of two opposing forms of life, which can never understand one another. The town and city, new, passing, ever-changing, sophisticated, cultured, but restless and unstable: the farm and countryside, old, established, unchanging, ignorant, uncultured, but steadfast and stable as the landscape itself. To the born and bred farmer and peasant the towns and cities are mere excrescences on the countryside covering so much good arable land. The townsman, on the other hand, cannot hope to cover the whole countryside with his buildings, for he realizes only too well his dependence on agriculture for his food. For all the wealth and power of civilization it is dependent upon the services of agriculture, and cannot exist without the primitive peasantry. While on the other hand, the agricultural community could continue to exist in the absence of civilization, and would, indeed, be all the more prosperous, when civilization lay in ruins, on account of the products it could retain rather than share them with the townspeople.

This truth is amply confirmed by the prosperity of agriculture in time of war, when civilizations are engaged in mutual destruction. Except where their lands are wasted by the contending armies the agriculturists reap wealth from the misfortunes of their fellow-citizens. Indeed, the worse the plight into which war throws civilization the greater the prosperity of the primitive agricultural partner in the scheme of things. During the recent war and subsequent economic disturbance, English farmers were successful enough, but in Germany, where the state suffered utter ruin, the countryside enjoyed such prosperity that nearly every village throughout the country has been half rebuilt and equipped with all modern conveniences, including electric light and power. The interests of agriculture and of civilization are essentially antagonistic, as are those of host and parasite. What harms and weakens the parasite must of necessity be of advantage to the host; when civilization suffers a set-back, agriculture enjoys unusual health, when civilization recovers, agriculture suffers a relapse. It is not surprising that more candid English farmers of an earlier day drank to 'A long war and a bloody one!' they knew instinctively where their interests lay.

When civilization comes into being it is controlled and directed by an omnipotent autocrat, who rules with despotic power by means of a bureaucracy of officials. He represents in his own person the superorganic reality of civilization, and claims as a right the surplus of agricultural production upon which civilization depends for nourishment. Economic conditions differ on that account very greatly in this early stage of civilization from what we are accustomed to consider economic in these later democratic times. The producers of food, materials, and articles of all kinds are regarded as servants of the state, and are permitted to retain only sufficient of their products to supply their simplest needs of life, while the surplus is claimed by the state, and collected by a rigorous form of taxation and control. The people are conceived as barbarians, which indeed they were at no distant date, and the state feels it has performed its duty when it has provided the same standard of life that they would have endured in the barbaric state. Any surplus of wealth that is produced by the co-operative organization of civilization is by right the property of the superorganism, that is, of the state and the autocrat himself. Hence an autocratic state from the economic point of view is a great centralized system, in which the palace and capital of the autocrat forms the focus, whether it be Memphis, Nineveh, Pataliputra, Kioto, Cusco, to mention only a few of the cities made famous by autocracy at the height of its power The entire surplus production of the empire, after the simplest needs of the inhabitants have been satisfied, pours as a vast tribute to the capital, where it is expended upon various cultural enterprises, as the autocrat and his government may direct. Such an autocracy is in no sense benevolent, but is occupied exclusively with the realization of super-organic aims. Such wealth as is collected from the people is never expended directly for their benefit as individuals, but is used to further the interests and growth of the super-organism, as a real higher entity.

The most striking form of economic centralization was apparently attained in Peru under the Incas, where such a perfect organization in the state service was established that it has been repeatedly mistaken by casual students for a condition of 'State Socialism.' Nothing could be more mistaken, if we interpret Socialism in its modern form of 'social service.' Peru was a perfect example of a centralized autocracy. The people worked in the common interest it is true, but they only received the bare necessities of life as their share of the product, and the surplus of their production went to construct the magnificent roads, palaces, and temples of the Inca Empire. The people, however, had no right to the use of these roads, palaces, and temples for their own purposes. They were state property, possessions of the holy Inca, and the famous post-runners themselves were only a form of governmental intercommunication, and in no sense a general postal system open to the public.

In other autocratic states, such as that of Assyria, a less exhaustive system of social organization is established, and the provinces and outlying peoples are compelled to support the state by a vast system of tribute imposed by military power. This is rather a degraded form of autocracy, as little endeavour is made to govern by organization, but only by force. Yet even in Assyria the scribe was an efficient official, and vast enforced migrations were carried out under his control, which are without parallel except in distant Peru many centuries later.

Finally, some autocracies, which are not so powerful or do not wield an unchallenged authority, as, for example, the Papacy in Europe, are content to leave production and commerce unembarrassed by state control, and gather their tribute by means of a high taxation of the product. Thus we have the 'tithes' imposed by the Catholic Church on the production of Christendom, a turnover tax of 10 per cent., which represents a far higher burden upon industry than any modern government would dare to inflict, even upon the agricultural lands and produce, from which the greater part of the medieval income was obtained.

After the autocrat has gathered together into his own hand the immense income that accrues from the surplus production of his whole empire, the question of its expenditure arises. First of all the bureaucratic administration of the state must be financed, and an adequate defence force supported, then the roads, barracks, and forts must be built and maintained, which are necessary to the existence and efficient administration of the empire. But even after this necessary expense of maintenance is deducted, the net revenue remains a huge yearly sum. The fruits of newly-established or re-established civilization accumulate rapidly in the treasury of the autocrat for expenditure at his direction. It is in the manner of the expenditure of this ultimate surplus that autocracy shows its essential dissimilarity from democracy. The accumulated revenues of autocracy have been deliberately levied from the subjects of the empire, and there is no intention to redistribute them in the form of social service. Such a policy is a late democratic innovation, and never even occurs to the leaders of autocratic government. The autocrat is the mortal representative of the superorganism on earth, and he is clearly authorized to apply his power, authority, and revenue to the realization of superorganic aims. The interests of the state are paramount on the economic as well as on the political plane.

There are two main directions in which economic expenditure may be applied in the interests of the super-organism. First and foremost the accumulated wealth of the state may be used to subsidize great wars of conquest and expansion against surrounding barbarian peoples and other neighbouring civilizations, in order to bring a greater amount of territory under the control of the autocrat. This has been the policy of many, if not of all, civilizations during their autocratic phase. We have only to think of the conquests of the XVIII Egyptian dynasty of the New Kingdom in Syria and Nubia; of the Assyrians in Armenia, Syria, and Egypt; of the Moguls in India; the Turks in Europe; not forgetting the Crusades of our own Papacy. Every autocracy has in greater or less degree engaged in foreign conquest, and some, like the Turks and Assyrians, have expended almost their entire resources upon military enterprises. It is clear that the expansion of the territory upon which the superorganism depends must be of advantage to civilization, and hence in engaging in military aggression the autocrat is furthering the interests of the superorganism in a very practical manner, and is fully justified in applying the revenue of the state to the cause of military glory.

After expending varying proportions of their total revenue upon military enterprise all autocracies spend the entire remainder upon various works to the glorification, both of the autocrat himself and of the godhead, which is the unconscious image of superorganic reality. Buildings and monuments are erected to glorify the ruler and the church. These far surpass in sheer magnificence, size, and beauty, the utilitarian structures of later phases of civilization, and are worthy records of the self-sacrifice and religious faith of early civilized communities. In this stage of civilization individuals realize the existence of a higher power over them and above them, to which they owe service, and the subjects of autocratic empire are eager to sacrifice their own economic interests to the erection of buildings of sufficient magnificence and splendour to glorify the ideals of civilization and of religion, which inspire their service. During the period of Papal ascendancy in Europe, the burghers of the squalid medieval towns were content to live in tumble-down hovels, that their God might be fittingly housed in a magnificent Gothic Church or Cathedral.

The amount of expenditure upon such non-utilitarian building of palaces, monuments, and temples must be strictly complementary to military expenditure, and we find in history that those autocracies which have been most warlike have produced least monumental building. Thus we have the Assyrians, whose great palaces and walled city at Nineveh are almost the sole relic of their grandeur, and the Turks, who concentrated to such a degree upon military operations that they have left scarcely any durable monuments to record their centuries of dominion.

Other autocrats, such as the Theban Pharaohs, the Moguls, the Popes, have engaged in moderate measure in wars of conquest, and have found time and economic resources to build wonderful monuments to the glorification of their regime. The glories of Karnak, the beautiful Taj Mahal, St. Peter's and the Vatican, all bear testimony to the monumental building of such autocracies.

It is, however, to the peaceful states in sheltered seclusion that we must turn for the real triumphs of monumental architecture—to Egypt of the early dynasties isolated in her desert sands, to Knossus secure in her island fastness, to Cusco high on her mountain ranges. There we find the most wonderful and astounding economic feats of building in comparison with the resources of the people who constructed them. In Egypt particularly the immense pyramids of Memphis remain to this day baffling mysteries, constructed as they were at the very dawn of civilization with the most primitive means.

The national states which take the place of autocratic empire in the oligarchic phase follow in a certain measure the economic model of autocracy, but the national monarchs are naturally less wealthy, commanding a smaller revenue than the former omnipotent autocrats. In the first place their national domains are but a small fraction of the widespread territories of autocratic empire, so that even if they were able to collect the whole surplus of production throughout their kingdom they could never hope to compete in grandeur with the autocrats of the former era of political unity. Furthermore, their authority is not the unhampered despotism of autocracy, but is restricted on every side by the newly-gained privileges of the oligarchic order. The surplus production of the lower orders is still levied as remorselessly as ever, but the state has no longer a monopoly of this revenue, being forced to share it with the newly arisen aristocratic caste. As the monarch only rules at the discretion of this caste, he is forced to maintain their privileges intact, and cannot apply taxation with the same rigour to them as to the common people. The former general levy upon the entire economic resources of the community is hence impossible, and the monarch is reduced to a much more restricted revenue. Nevertheless, the national exchequer can still command very considerable wealth, and this is expended exactly as is the revenue of autocracy, exclusively upon the glorification of the monarch and of the state, and upon military enterprise in the furtherance of national interests.

Thus we have Louis XIV gathering together the economic resources of France, despite the exemption of the nobles and clergy from taxation, and embarking upon his vast wars of conquest in the Netherlands and Germany, while he still found sufficient funds to build his wonderful palace of Versailles. Other European monarchs have followed his example in greater or less degree, and while their mutual wars devastated Europe their palaces and castles rose in competitive splendour in every capital city.

In ancient Greece the same economic expenditure may be traced in the budgets of the city states, although, indeed, upon a more exalted plane. Athens, too, at the height of her glory spent her revenues partly upon her Homeric struggle for the hegemony of Greece, and partly upon the adornment of the city to the glorification of Athena; and of the state.

In the oligarchic phase the luxury of the emancipated aristocratic caste becomes of the highest economic importance. A very large part of the economic energies of the whole people is deflected from the service of the state to the gratification of the luxurious tastes of the oligarchs. When we speak of surplus production we do not necessarily mean that the people produce more than they require of the simple necessities of life alone. We mean that a small number of the people are able to produce sufficient of the simple necessities of life for the whole community, and the remainder of the people are available to produce other articles, undertake military operations, or erect buildings and fortifications as may be required. Under autocracy this surplus of labour is all appropriated by the state for the furtherance of the aims of the superorganism, but in the oligarchic phase a large and ever-increasing proportion is applied to the production of luxuries for the oligarchic caste. The extremely luxurious life of oligarchic castes throughout the world is really too well known for any great need of reference here.

The luxury of the French court of Louis XIV and Louis XV was notorious, but even in England during the eighteenth century a very great amount of luxury was enjoyed by the upper classes.

Further afield, the Manchus in China enjoyed a most magnificent and luxurious seclusion in their racial settlements, as did the British for many decades in India.

The Japanese Samurai, despite their frugal traditions, maintained a high standard of life.

In more distant times the Greeks were not less luxurious, although more stress has been laid upon their culture than upon their mode of life.

As the oligarchic caste establishes and confirms its position of ascendance in society, its demand for luxuries of all kinds to maintain its high standard of life entirely alters the economic complexion of civilization. The extreme centralization of tribute flowing from all parts of a huge empire to one great economic focus is entirely changed, not only on account of national disruption, which tends to substitute new local centres of taxation, but because of the oligarchic demand for new forms of production for the gratification of luxurious caste tastes. The absolute control and direction of production asserted by autocracy is renounced, and for the first time individual demand and supply begin to determine economic organization. Not only production, but trade also, is released from state control and becomes of vital economic importance. The luxurious caste of oligarchy soon acquires an exotic taste in foreign articles drawn from strange peoples and civilization far afield. Merchant vessels face the perils of the seas on great voyages, merchant caravans toil through the unending plains and deserts, to bring the exotic luxuries, precious stones, and curiosities of the far corners of the earth to the privileged homes of aristocracy. Oligarchy encourages trade to arise once more after the deadening commercial centralization of autocracy is past.

We have only to turn to the highly commercial Greeks of the classical period, with their network of trade routes over land and sea, to realize how fully a cultural oligarchic community may become engaged in trading enterprise.

In classical China, similarly, the Contending States engaged in such extensive commercial enterprise that Chinese iron was known and highly praised on the distant Roman market.

In Europe, we have the Venetians and Genoese bearing in their ships from the Levant and Black Sea the products of the waning civilization of the Near East to the patrician palaces of the Lombard plain; the Hanseatic traders buying the products of the Far East in the markets of Great Novgorod, whither they had been gathered by many a weary caravan journey through the steppes and deserts of Central Asia from the unknown civilizations of India and China.

In conditions of national disruption, however, certain trade restrictions are inevitable on account of the necessity of each state maintaining its national independence. The great struggle for the hegemony of civilization is not only fought out by force of arms in the sharp clashes of periodic wars, the contest proceeds as determinedly and fiercely on the economic side in the intervening periods of peace. Each nation or city-state seeks trading posts, markets, commercial concessions, and spheres of influence, from which it attempts to exclude its rivals and to exploit to its own advantage and enrichment alone. It is here a matter of complete indifference to each state that the restrictions upon international trade which it imposes are contrary to the general interests of civilization as a whole. The struggle of nation against nation for the hegemony of civilization is continuous and stubborn, and no nation will lay down its weapons, either military, naval, or economic, as long as the conflict continues and the hegemony remains unattained. Each nation will continue to maintain its restrictions upon foreign competition within its own country, and in the lands under its control, as a means of frustrating its opponents and, relatively, advancing its own interests; and any attempt to bring about economic disarmament will be found as difficult and as stubbornly resisted by independent national states as military disarmament itself. National disruption is in itself an unnatural and chaotic, if inevitable, phase of civilization, and as essentially and fundamentally a continuous state of conflict, military in time of 'war' and economic in time of 'peace.'

The great difficulties placed in the way of the recent endeavour to bring about a 'Tariff Truce' in Europe illustrate very clearly the continuance of war conditions on the economic plane. The lack of sympathy on the part of France for economic assistance for Germany still more recently is another example.

Where a hegemony is eventually attained all trade restrictions fall away as a matter of course, and the reunited oligarchic imperialism will generally adopt 'free trade' as its motto in its commercial relations with the rest of the world.

When Great Britain attained her hegemony of the seas in the late eighteenth century, she lost her interest in the land hegemony of the European continent, and soon found it to her advantage to enter into 'free trade' relations with the rest of the world. The existence of 'free trade' in Great Britain is a clear indication of the escape of this country from the narrow nationalism of the Continent.

When oligarchic caste supremacy is broken in the throes of democratic revolution, a complete reorganization of economic structure takes place. The whole substance of autocratic and oligarchic economics is based upon the assumption that the majority of the community is content to live at the lowest limit of bare subsistence in the service of the state. With the advent of democracy, however, the lower orders of the civilized community are no longer willing to shoulder all the burden of civilization without a commensurate share of its benefits. The producing class insist upon a greater and greater share of the product which they cultivate or manufacture, and various forms of pressure are brought to bear by the working class to raise their wages from the earlier minimum of actual bodily subsistence to a level which permits of a share in the simpler luxuries of civilization. At the same time they no longer offer the same long hours of labour, even for enhanced wages, but claim greater leisure in order to enjoy the luxuries of life which they now claim. This is obviously a revolutionary change in economic organization, and has the effect of reducing to a minimum the excess of production over wage costs, which was the peculiarity of earlier economic life. A much greater percentage of the cost of an article in democratic times is made up of the wages which must be paid to the workers who produce it, and a very much smaller percentage is available for government expenditure and oligarchic extravagance.

The luxury of the oligarchic caste comes to an abrupt end, and with it the demand for luxuries and exotic curiosities dies away. A new demand arises in its place, financed by the large wage-earning capacity of the emancipated lower orders, and calls for greater supplies of the necessities of life and the simpler luxuries. Production becomes reorganized to supply this new demand, and makes up in quantity, low price, and quick turnover for the former trade in quality, high prices, and long credits to the account of oligarchy. Mass production becomes the commercial slogan, and meets the changed conditions of the times. It is no longer the state or a limited caste that is taking the excess production of civilization, but the whole people.

We are passing through just such a revolutionary economic crisis in this country at the present time. Most remarkable has been the astounding success of all industries which supply simple luxuries to the masses at low prices, as compared with the depressed state of other trades. Cheap motor cars, artificial silk, cigarettes, gramophones, have all proved extraordinarily profitable articles, and tremendous, unprecedented booms have swelled these industries to immense proportions. When the production of civilization is turned to the gratification of the whole people, it is soon found that the individual share is not so large as might have been expected. Autocracy, and in minor degree oligarchy, have only been able to attain their effects of power and wealth by a concentration of the whole communal resources. When this concentration is redistributed as democracy requires, it is clear that from the point of view of the individualist civilization is after all no such very great improvement upon barbarism in the amount of individual income it produces. Civilization owes its apparent wealth and power to the superorganic co-operation of its members, and if these human members insist upon economically disintegrating civilization, it is surprising how little actually falls to each individual. This unfortunate fact is soon brought to popular notice, and the immediate reaction is to introduce more efficient methods of production in order to increase the general income in the individual's favour. The people who had remained uninterested in the improvement of the obsolete and inefficient methods of production of their fathers as long as the greater part of the product went either to the government or to a privileged caste, take the greatest interest in finding better and more productive methods when the greater part of the fruits of their labour return to them as wages. Ingenious inventions are made in rapid sequence, and rationalized methods of manufacture and cultivation are introduced.

In the early stages of democratic revolution the working classes are inclined to favour some form of socialistic control of industry, in order to safeguard their interests against any recrudescence of oligarchic oppression. An outcry is raised against capitalist extortion, which is only justified as long as capitalism is imbued with the oligarchic principle of forcing the lower orders to serve their 'betters.' In time, however, the capitalists find that their own interests are best served in themselves giving service to the people as a whole, as Henry Ford has demonstrated beyond any further argument in recent times. Furthermore, such efforts of nationalization and state control of industry as are attempted by democracy invariably prove futile and costly failures. Finally, the workers and the democratic community generally recognize the need of expert and efficient leadership in industry if a large return in the form of production and hence of wages is to be obtained. Communal control having proved hopelessly inefficient, and the common people being determined at all costs to increase the rate of wages to a more comfortable level, the democratic community deliberately hands over its economic destinies to the industrial capitalists. The great ideals of democratic 'liberty' and 'equality' which had inspired the revolution against aristocratic tyranny are thus bartered away for a 'mess of pottage,' and democracy sells its birthright to plutocracy for a general higher standard of life.

The last economic phase of civilization is thus reached, when the plutocratic leaders of industry take control of commercial organization. They fulfil their bargain faithfully with democracy by advancing the efficiency of production to a high level and raising wages; and hence the general standard of life of the community varies considerably: but in return they claim their pound of flesh. Their expert knowledge and efficiency are worth a large reward to democracy, and this reward is paid with all munificence. Furthermore, democratic law has raised the possession of property and the assessment of interest to absolute legal rights of almost holy potency, and the economic knowledge and power of these commercial dictators enable them to amass immense fortunes which are passed on from generation to generation to breed more wealth. Thus the personal wealth of plutocracy gathers substance like a rolling snowball, until the whole of the capital of the entire community has fallen into a few hands. This was the final stage of the Roman Empire, when the veteran farmers were finally displaced and the land as the source of wealth had all passed into the hands of the plutocratic plantation owners. It is already approaching realization in America, where millionaires of unprecedented personal wealth are gaining an ever-increasing control of the economic organization of the United States of America. When the process reaches its culmination, democracy is delivered entirely into the power of plutocracy, and the authority of the latter is so firmly established on the very foundations of democratic society, that it can only be overturned by the complete destruction of material civilization in its entirety.

Thus we find that the democratic principle of usury supported by the 'justice' of democratic law leads to a personal triumph of individualism over civilization, so that the whole wealth and power of the entire superorganism falls into a few hands. As these last plutocratic proprietors of civilization have not the slightest conception of super-organic idealism, being inevitably atheistic realists only interested in making as great a personal profit as possible out of their immense possessions, the end is obviously in sight. It was not for nothing that the Catholic Church in the Middle Ages forbade usury as contrary to the dictates of God; the Papacy was highly inspired with superorganic idealism and appreciated quite clearly, if unconsciously, that the personal interests of the individual must run counter to those of the superorganism, and that hence it was contrary to superorganic interests to allow an individual to accumulate great personal wealth at the expense of the community. The final conclusion of civilization, as the personal possession of a handful of financiers, certainly confirms the wisdom of Papal policy.

Barbarian invasion naturally puts an end to economic prosperity, and the rage of the slave element towards the economic bondage which they have suffered finds an outlet in the complete destruction of all economic machinery. All normal trade and commerce comes to a complete standstill, and the extinction of civilization is nowhere so complete and disastrous as on the economic plane. The enormous accumulation of wealth during the plutocratic era cannot, however, be annihilated over-night: indeed the invasion of the barbarian tribes has been largely inspired by their desire of possessing themselves of this great wealth. The migrating tribes march from city to city laden with the spoils of their conquests.

Actually a new and unnatural trade has been on occasion based upon the exchange and barter of this loot of an extinct civilization with other barbarian tribes farther afield, and with distant civilizations unaffected by the barbarian inroads. In this strange trade between ignorant barbarians and sophisticated civilized merchants the strangest anomalies arise. On the one hand the barbarians have an immense superfluity of those articles of luxury that civilization values most highly, and on the other they lack, through their destruction of civilized industry and cultivation, those simple necessities of life which the distant civilization possesses in bulk and values scarcely at all. Under these circumstances the incentive to active trade exists in the most intense form, and a great part of the loot of the extinct civilization passes to existing civilizations at a distance in exchange for those necessities which the barbarians crave.

The most striking example of this form of sterile trade is to be found in the medieval period, when the Mongols had crushed both the Caliphate and the Chinese Empire, and held sway from the borders of Christendom to the Pacific Ocean. The Mongols had gathered the most extraordinary collection of loot and plunder from the innumerable cities and towns they had taken and sacked throughout Asia and Eastern Europe. Not content with the mere possession of this immense accumulation of sterile wealth, the Mongols learned to barter a part of it with the extant civilizations of Europe and India in exchange for necessities and manufactured goods which they lacked and hence valued more highly. It was this unnatural and hence temporary trade that laid the foundations of the great commercial federations of medieval Europe. Caravans toiled across the steppes and deserts of Central Asia and Russia to carry Mongol loot to Great Novgorod, there to be bartered for European manufactures, and a chain of Hansa cities carried the trade farther down the Baltic to Western Europe. Similarly, in the South, the Mongol caravans reached the Mediterranean in Syria, and a great trade was carried on with the Venetian and Genoese merchants, who then shipped the goods to Italy and the West. It is obvious that a trade of this kind can only last until the accumulation of looted wealth is exhausted, although the trade routes once opened between civilization and civilization may continue to function on a reduced scale as normal channels of commerce. Hence the decline of the Hanseatic League, and of Venice and Genoa, had its origin in the exhaustion of the Mongol plunder and the collapse of Mongol world power, and was not primarily the result of the discovery of America and the ocean route to the Indies.

THE ECONOMIC CYCLE

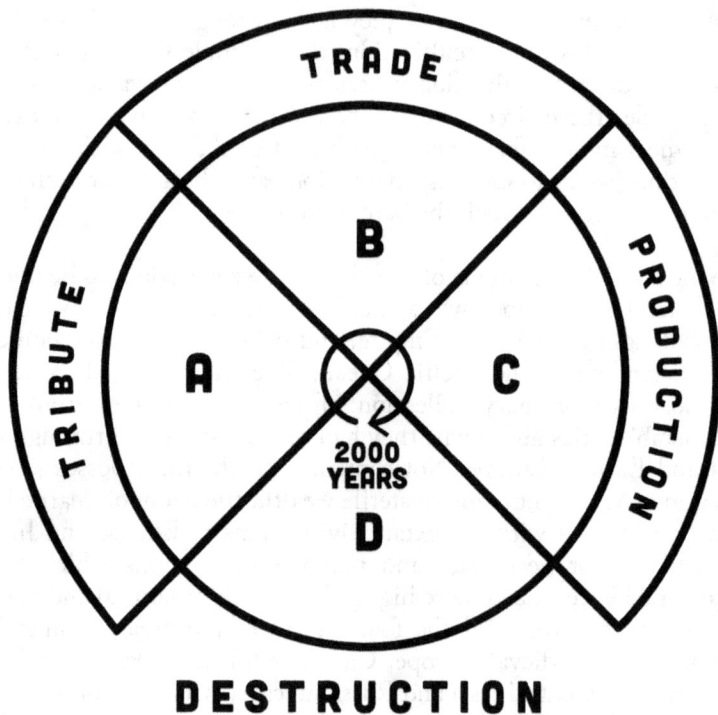

This cycle is obviously allied to the foregoing political one, although it would be difficult to state which was the dominant influence and determined the other. We can only claim a general interdependence of political and economic factors. Here again there is an obvious 'nadir' in quadrant D, but the zenith is more easily determined from a purely materialistic point of view, as the productive era in quadrant C undoubtedly piles up an immense amount of wealth. Hence from the economic standpoint the greatest triumphs of democratic production closely precede the final destruction of the entire economic apparatus. The prosperity of an advanced democracy like the United States of America is, in fact, an ominous feature with regard to the future of American civilization.

Chapter 5

The Social Cycle

In the state of barbarism which precedes the advent of civilization an essential equality of social status is the real basis of tribal life. For evidence of this equality we cannot do better than turn to the earliest records of the Anglo-Saxon tribes which invaded England and expelled the Romanized Britons at the dawn of our history.

We find in the social organization of these tribes democratic customs and institutions which, after an intermediate period of eclipse, have only been restored within the last century; and there is every reason to believe that these democratic features were a common attribute of all nomadic life, as we can trace similar customs recorded in the early Vedic legends of the Aryan tribes which invaded India a thousand years and more before the Anglo-Saxons reached England. Thus we find that the latter tribes held a considerable part of their land in common, and their 'commons' still exist as communal pasture-land here and there in the country, despite the 'enclosures' of oligarchic landowners. They also elected their tribal leaders, much as our modern republics elect their presidents, and only finally submitted to hereditary monarchy when the Norman invasion imposed a foreign dynasty upon the Anglo-Saxon nation. What is more, the people had a definite share in their own government, as is evidenced by the Witenagemots of the Anglo-Saxons, which early councils laid the seeds of self-government, that later bore fruit in the first true English parliaments.

The grounds for accepting these highly democratic or socialistic tendencies in Anglo-Saxon England as an indication of general primitive nomadic conditions of life elsewhere are very strong, on account of the fact that it was in England alone that the Teutonic barbarians who invaded the Roman Empire actually massacred the Romanized population or drove them into Wales, Cornwall, and Brittany. There was none of the intermingling with the Latin population as was general throughout Gaul, Spain, and Italy, and we may well assume that up to the time of the inroads of the Norsemen there was no purer Teutonic community anywhere in Europe. The stubborn resistance of the English to the spread of Christianity, which was so readily adopted by the other Teutonic tribes, is also sure evidence of the purity of their barbaric tradition. It was only with the

Norman Conquest that the assimilation of England into the European system, with its Latin culture, was finally completed.

The equality of social status that was a feature of the Anglo-Saxon tribes is no matter for surprise, where no differentiation of function was known. As a pastoral people each man was a herdsman and a warrior, and it was only especial merit in the common task that deserved reward. In war they chose some man of particular valour to be their leader, but even this leader joined in the fighting with his own arms, as there was little, if any, attempt at strategic operations requiring generalship. Furthermore, the tribe was never foolish enough to allow such an office of leadership to become hereditary, as the importance of real bravery and personal character was much too vital to be left to chance. If the son of a former chief inherited some of his father's greatness, then well and good, but if he was a degenerate weakling the tribe would never tolerate his command, and would make use of its power of election to place a more worthy man in his stead. Equality was, of course, no slavish artificial equality such as we know in these degenerate times, as each man was expected to show himself worthy of a place in the common councils of his tribe. A practical equality of opportunity, however, existed for any man of outstanding merit in the common activities of the tribe, regardless of his birth or origin. In fact, a nomadic barbarian tribe as a static biological entity had long since evolved the most efficient form of social organization for its primitive purposes, and, as in a wolfpack, leadership was delegated to the strongest individual in the tribe, subject to the approval of the community as a whole. With the advent of the autocratic phase of civilization, there is little change in the social organization of the former barbarian tribes as such. Equality of tribal status becomes an equality of service to the new cultural autocracy. The former tribal leaders may in some cases survive, but then only in the form of anachronisms, highly antagonistic to the progress of civilization. Such were typically the robber barons of Germany during the Middle Ages, raiding from a backwater of history the trade of the free Hanseatic cities. Later these barbaric leaders may come into their own again, when the disruptive tendencies that prove fatal to autocratic unity eventually restore local tribal or national loyalties, but for a time they are under the eclipse of all-powerful autocratic authority.

One section of the community alone is elevated above the general barbaric level, and this elevation is in no sense artificial, having its basis in a real cultural superiority over the common people. This section it is that possesses a monopoly of the cultural inspiration of dawning civilization, and forms the bureaucratic administration of the autocratic state. Such were the Scribes of Assyria, the Priests of the Papacy, the Ulema in the Sultanate, who were the only really literate people in their respective systems. This bureaucracy is enthroned high above the common people in popular estimation, owing to the fact that it alone possesses that culture towards which the former barbarians show such respect. Its members speak a learned tongue unintelligible to the laity, Babylonian, Latin, Arabic, bearing the inspiration of culture from foregoing civilization. They are, furthermore, dressed in impressive vestments, which distinguish them from the generality of unenlightened subjects of empire.

Modern analogy would suggest that this superior cultured class of bureaucratic administrators of government must become a hereditary caste passing its privileges from father to son, generation after generation. Nothing could, in point of fact, be farther from the truth. Far from the bureaucratic administration passing from father to son, in the case of several religious bureaucracies marriage is actually denied to the priest-administrators, and in all cases hereditary principles are entirely neglected. The autocracy is at pains to select its bureaucrats from among the most talented subjects of the empire. Youths of ability are chosen, quite regardless of their social standing, from among the common people, and educated in the free governmental schools of the administration. Should they prove sufficiently gifted to satisfy their superiors in examination or otherwise, they are then passed direct into the administration, and form the next generation of bureaucrats. Education is in no sense universal; there is no attempt to educate the people as a whole. Certain picked individuals are instructed in the art of government. Autocratic education is restricted to the preparation and examination of candidates for the vast civil service of the autocratic state.

In course of time culture passes by degrees from the administrative bureaucracy of autocracy to the more enlightened sections of the common people. Finally the great autocratic administration is broken, and its monopoly of culture destroyed. As culture must still, as always, be the source of government, the cultured class, despite their greater dispersion, band together to undertake the administration of the disrupted national units of the former empire. They elect local temporal rulers, choosing frequently the descendants of former tribal leaders, who have been for a time eclipsed by autocratic splendour. Under these local rulers they form the administration of the new national states, reproducing in miniature in each state the former centralized government of autocracy. We find that in every case government office has become the exclusive privilege of a hereditary class. In England to this day the son of a ploughman may become a priest of the Church of Rome, but by no means a clergyman of the Church of England, and but fifty years ago he could inconceivably have held government office, however great his ability. A great social cleavage of society distinguishes the nationalist age from the foregoing era of autocracy and the following era of democracy. During this period the natural equality of opportunity is denied, and class distinctions based upon birth intervene.

It is very important to realize that this is a passing and comparatively short-lived phase of civilization, for as we are just emerging from such a period of European history at the present day, we are too apt to conceive that this social cleavage of high-born and lowborn is a natural and universal attribute of human organization. Actually it is highly unnatural and artificial, unknown to primitive society and to the greater part of civilized history. It was to this instinctive appreciation of 'natural' law that both the American and French revolutionaries appealed, when they propounded the 'natural' rights of all men to equality, that is, to the equality of opportunity.

As the division of society into high-born and low-born according to the precepts of the caste system is highly artificial, except where the division follows sharply defined racial lines, means have to be devised by the dominant caste to distinguish themselves quite clearly from the common people. The simplest and most obvious method is to decree some outward and visible sign of superiority that is denied to the lower classes. Some distinctive form of dress has been almost universally adopted as a means of denoting the rank of a member of a dominant caste, and the right of bearing weapons has also played an important role. As in the absence of strongly marked racial differences there is, despite aristocratic belief to the contrary, very little actual physical distinction between the high- and low-born, laws with severe penalties have to be decreed to prevent low-born 'impostors' from wearing the dress only permitted to their superiors, and gaining thereby entrance into exclusive caste society. Such laws which impose standards of dress upon the various classes of the community are termed 'Sumptuary Laws,' and may be traced throughout the civilized world.

At the height of the nationalist oligarchic period in Europe during the eighteenth century distinctions of dress between the aristocracy and the common people reached a great height, and in the French Revolution the extremists deliberately termed themselves 'Sansculottes' to mark their hatred of the high-born wearers of silk knee-breeches. This period is also marked by the right of wearing swords, which was the monopoly of the aristocratic gentleman.

At exactly the same time in far distant Japan very similar conditions prevailed, and it is interesting to note that the Samurai gentleman was also distinguished from the common people by his right of wearing a sword, like his European prototype, only he was not content with one sword, but wore two at the same time.

In India to this day the utmost complexity of costume marks the traditional caste system of the land, which has survived almost unimpaired the half-hearted Moslem intervention in the Middle Ages, and this outward diversity of costume is a visible sign of that diversity of opinion that delays the restoration of native Indian rule. Until the Indians learn to dress alike, the British Raj will prevail.

Social cleavage may be outwardly expressed in the reverse manner by imposing some degrading costume upon the lower orders, while leaving the dominant caste freedom to develop their own taste in dress free of restriction.

The most interesting and characteristic example of this form of distinction is to be found in recent Chinese history. When the Manchus invaded and conquered China, they imposed a racial oligarchic caste government upon the country, but there was little actual physical difference in appearance between Manchu and Chinese. Hence means were taken to intensify such racial distinctions as actually existed. The invaders, being a more primitive stock from the northern wilds of Manchuria, regarded the cultured and over-civilized people of the south as an effeminate race, while recognizing their intellectual powers, and emphasized by a prescribed fashion of head-dress the physical attributes of intellect and effeminacy. A high forehead is the hallmark of brains east or west, and the 'highbrow' Chinese differed markedly from the 'lowbrow' Manchu in this particular alone. Hence this difference was deliberately accentuated to Manchu order by compelling all the Chinese to shave their hair off the forehead as far as the crown of the head, thus making of the subject-people a race of artificial 'highbrows.' After paying tribute to their greater intellect, the Manchus proceeded to lay emphasis upon the comparative degeneration of the Chinese by decreeing that the subject-people wear their hair long in a pigtail down the back, as a sign of womanly weakness. The result was that during the rule of the Manchus it was always possible at a glance to distinguish between subject and ruling caste. Whenever the Chinese rose in revolt against the Manchu, the first thing they did was to allow their hair to grow on the front of the head and to cut off their pigtails.

A further artificial, if higher, method of promoting the ascendancy of the dominant caste is by the inculcation of a code of honour, and by the observance of certain conventions of conduct and behaviour. In world history many such codes have been developed in widely separated regions, varying in merit from the high idealist ceremonial of Confucius to the harsh barbaric code of honour of the German army officer. All are alike in imposing an arbitrary ceremonial upon human intercourse, which has little, if any, relation to natural functioning, and is mainly improvised to draw an artificial distinction between the well-bred, 'who know how to behave,' and the ignorant populace, who are without manners. Convention is not devised to forbid or restrict natural functioning, but to give a ceremonial cloak to mere crude natural instinct, and to distinguish thereby the 'cultivated' man, who has been brought up in the code, from the 'uncultivated' natural man, who either has never learned or deliberately neglects to bow to the conventional standards of the dominant caste.

Confucius built up the most amazing structure of ceremonial by means of which the correct behaviour for every conceivable occasion was rigidly defined. We must admit a certain symbolic beauty in much of this Confucian ritual, but we must not fail to recognize the extreme conventionalism of his system with its extravagant artificiality. The very complexity of this code was such that only men of leisure and studious nature could hope to master all its intricacies, with the result that Confucian ceremonial has become the test of social standing in China, and the ability to know the correct behaviour in all possible eventualities of everyday life the hallmark of caste distinction, the sign of the attainment of the standard of Confucius's 'superior man' who had triumphed over crude natural instinct. It is not surprising that the ruling caste in the oligarchic phases of both Early and Late Chinese Civilizations should have clung with great tenacity to Confucianism, and that the recent dominant Manchus were confirmed Confucians.

The Far East would seem to be the home of excessive ceremonial, as in Japan during the Samurai oligarchy a similar but quite distinct code of conduct was evolved, which reached the extreme and extraordinary artificial conventionalism that a mother would give a laugh of politeness in telling of the death of a favourite son.

It would, however, be a great mistake to assume that European Civilization is free of such artificial conventionalism, although admittedly the cruder European mind has never developed such extreme ceremonial as the more polished Oriental. Nevertheless, the Court life of the French monarchy at its height, and modern German officialdom, not to speak of Victorian England, have each attained in their time a considerable complexity of convention, and each has looked down upon the uninitiated in the mysteries of their ritual with an equal disdain. Even today, when oligarchy is rapidly giving place to democracy throughout Northern Europe, social distinctions based upon convention still persist. No more crushing condemnation is known to a certain class of Englishman than to term a man a 'bounder,' which merely means that he offends in some quite minor degree against the conventional code of the speaker's class. Returning to a sartorial illustration, to appear at a hunt meet clad in incorrectly cut riding breeches is a much more heinous crime than to run off with the young wife of the huntsman himself, provided the latter operation is carried out in the style proper to the occasion.

The code of honour itself, which seems as the laws of the Medes and Persians to its aristocratic adherents, is as artificial a product of caste interests, and proves on a little examination one of the chief bulwarks of caste ascendancy.

If a German officer of the late imperial army was insulted by a common soldier, his code of honour compelled him to run the offender through the body with his sword on the spot, but in behaving in this inhuman manner the officer was not, as he thought, protecting his personal 'honour,' a most flimsy artificial growth; he was inculcating in a most practical and bloodthirsty manner respect for the military caste among the lower orders of the imperial community.

We find that the Samurai of distant Japan had a very similar method of extorting the respect due to them from the lower orders, and one of the first 'incidents' that occurred upon the opening of Japan to foreign intercourse was when the Samurai of a Daimyo's bodyguard summarily despatched two foreigners who were guilty in all ignorance of an act of disrespect to their patron.

Similarly, the English public schoolboy's motto of 'never telling tales out of school' has proved invaluable in protecting the dominant caste against attack by 'outsiders,' as is aptly illustrated in Galsworthy's Loyalties.

Of course, some high standards of moral value are interwoven in the code of honour of the gentleman, or of any other similar caste, but we will find that the outstanding tenets of the code upon which most stress are laid have their origin in the support of caste ascendancy over the common people.

Despite the determined effort of the oligarchic caste to maintain its cultural privileges by the various means outlined above, culture does nevertheless spread gradually to the lower classes, who eventually rise in protest against caste prerogatives and conventional class distinctions. This revolt is generally of a violent nature, and has been termed 'revolution.' It involves the overturning of conventional standards and the liberation of thought and conduct from the artificial restrictions of class-conscious oligarchy. It restores the natural equality of opportunity denied for a time by caste privilege, and opens to the whole community a general communion in the cultural inspiration of civilization. Although violent convulsions, such as the French and Russian Revolutions, accompany this general democratic revolt against oligarchic privilege, yet the whole movement is too immense to be fully accomplished in such an upheaval of society, and is generally consummated by a widespread process of change, which gradually transforms society from its oligarchic mould to a true democracy.

European civilization is at present passing through this phase of 'general revolution,' which is now reaching its final culmination after the successive disturbances of the French Revolution, 1848, and the Russian Revolution. The immense and rapid changes that we may all note about us in these stirring times are not signs of the rapid forward progress of modern society aided by modern science; they are merely signs of a 'revolutionary' change of society from one stable form to another according to a principle of civilized development that may be traced in past eras of history, and even in contemporary events elsewhere.

At the present day Japan and China are both passing through a similar stage in their cultural development, and may yet lead Europe in democratic progress.

As this process of passing from an oligarchic to a democratic organization of society is actually going on before our very eyes, it may be best illustrated from contemporary social life. The most striking change in social affairs during the last decades, and especially since the German War, has been the decline of the strict conventions of the past 'Victorian' era, and their replacement by the shocking 'bad manners' of the younger generation, which greatly offend their elders born in the tradition of an era of graceful ceremony. Yet these bad manners' are merely an example of natural as distinct from artificial, conduct, and express the revolt of youth against the restrictions of a waning tradition. We find on all sides the most extraordinary difference in the respect, or lack of respect, professed by modern man towards the sacrosanct traditions and conventions of the past. We live in these days in a flux, and society is being melted down and recast. In this process of melting down, the familiar, if grotesque, forms of conventional caste morality are rapidly disappearing in the formless molten mass of democratic society. Old lamps are at a discount-new lamps are not yet at our disposal.

Yet there is nothing so utterly inexplicable in these social changes of our times. They merely usher in the coming era of democracy. As long as conventions and artificial codes of honour separate and distinguish, as we have seen, the initiated and privileged few, who possess the advantages of a good 'upbringing,' from the many, who have neither the leisure nor opportunity to learn the 'monkey tricks' of high society, democratic equality, however much it may be professed in theory, can never be accomplished in practice It is a perfectly natural and healthy process in the life-course of civilization when society deliberately uproots and destroys the last barriers to social equality, which encumber the ground and prevent the accomplishment of true democratic freedom of equality for all. As long as 'good manners,' a caste dialect like the 'Oxford accent,' correct dress and other monopolies of a caste upbringing, remain important factors in a young man's career, it is impossible to speak of true democracy. All artificial distinctions of this sort, which are of no real importance in affairs, are mere relics of oligarchic exclusiveness, and must be finally eradicated before democracy can come into its own. As we all know, such abilities, formerly of paramount importance, are rapidly passing from assets to liabilities in the individual struggle for success. Democracy, if not yet fully realized, has at least dawned in modern society.

Actually the advent of democracy does not by any means entail an equality of all in the new form of society. It is true that social distinctions based upon birth, breeding, or race are done away with, but this does not make human beings equal. Artificial inequalities may be removed, but natural inequalities remain. Even the most fanatical socialist has to admit that human beings are born with an amazing inequality of physique and mental ability. In order to attain the ideal of socialist equality we must impose still more artificial standards upon society. We find, for example, that modern Trade Unions in an endeavour to realize a form of social equality actually tend to restrict the output of the best and most efficient worker to that of the worst and least efficient. As these same Trade Unions follow the doctrine of Karl Marx that all wealth is the product of labour alone, we come immediately up against a paradox, which is even more absurd than the half-truth of heredity upon which caste rule is founded. Democracy, however, in its endeavour to advance the general income to the highest possible level, soon abandons any such restrictive devices, and the most democratic nation of the modern world— the U.S.A.—is the greatest enemy of socialist teaching, which it suppresses with all the violence of a persecution.

If equality of opportunity in democracy meant an equality of opportunity to serve the community or civilization, each according to his own abilities, natural inequalities of physique and mental powers would not be of very vital importance. They would merely mean the distribution of the various duties of service to the community in accordance with the inherent abilities of the various members of the community. Democracy, however, has almost entirely lost this fine, early instinct of service, and each member of the community only struggles to attain the greatest possible advantage over his fellows in the possession and distribution of the products of civilization. Service is no longer rendered with perfect lack of self-interest, and society can only enlist the efforts of the democratic citizen in return for a liberal material reward or promise of reward. While the ideal of the bureaucracy of early autocracy was to serve the state with complete self-sacrifice—and it was only with the passing of this ideal that autocracy collapsed—democracy begins from the very first to offer the most immense fortunes to those that render service to the community in the development of industrial organization. The point of view toward civilization has entirely changed, for while the subjects of autocratic empire rendered their service to the state as a matter of course, and the subjects of the nationalist states of the oligarchic era sacrificed their lives in mutual patriotic conflict, the citizens of democratic empire expect to enjoy all the fruits of civilization with the minimum of service to the superorganism. Hence inequalities of natural abilities in the social and commercial intercourse of democratic society lead almost immediately to the utmost material inequality of individual wealth, as each individual claims the utmost possible reward from the community for whatever service he may render it.

Democratic 'equality of opportunity' leads thus within a very few generations to the greatest inequality of rich and poor. America as the only firmly established modern democracy is also the home of millionaires and of some of the most miserable slums in the world. The Roman Empire was notorious for its extortionate capitalists and its many-storied slums in the suburbs of Rome. More important still is the fact that the right of inheritance of wealth from one generation to another invalidates the original 'equality of opportunity,' and enables the wealth of the rich to breed more wealth, while the poor are denied by degrees all hope of rising from their misery, however great their individual abilities may be. A new caste of plutocrats is evolved, which is much less tolerable than the former artificial caste of oligarchy, as it possesses a real material power of maintenance in its inherited wealth. In its endeavour to escape from social inequality, democracy has instituted a material inequality much harder to bear. In European civilization the distinction, Rich and Poor, is really of quite recent date as a vital division of society. It follows upon the distinctions, Clergy and Laity, of the Middle Ages, and Aristocrat and Burgher, of the Nationalist era, and is a vital indication of the materialist trend of modern society. We are apt to think of Rich and Poor as a natural and inevitable social distinction throughout history, largely on account of Jesus saying, 'The Poor we have always with us'; but we must not forget that Jesus himself lived in the dawn of a democratic epoch, when the Roman capitalists were extorting vast sums from the Near East.

Soon after the state of plutocracy is fully established, with its grave inequalities of individual wealth, civilization begins to decline. The cause of this decline lies not so much in the actual presence of plutocratic conditions as in the materialistic attitude towards civilization adopted by the democratic community. Instead of applying their energies to the service and advancement of the superorganism, the citizens of the democratic state desire to deflect the super-being from its higher aims to the service of its own puny constituent human cells. It is obvious that this purely negative attitude of the constituent members of civilization must inevitably have a deleterious effect upon the superorganism, and if persisted in will lead to a disintegration of civilization as a whole. The return to pure individualism is a denial of cultural co-operation, and foreshadows a return to barbarism. We see this process in full swing in modern America, where gangs of gunmen can defy the laws of the community, and amass personal wealth at the expense of their fellow-citizens. Here is a process of disintegration in full swing, when it becomes evident that it is more profitable to grab the fruits of civilization at the point of a revolver rather than to cultivate them as the reward of patient labour. Barbarism as the rule of might rather than of right is rapidly reclaiming America despite the grandiloquent pride of the Americans in their material prosperity.

Accompanying this intrinsic cause of cultural decline we find a natural revulsion of the dispossessed proletariat against 'capitalist' plutocracy. The proletariat has come to regard civilization as a form of slavery to materialist plutocracy, which it finds an intolerable burden. Here lies the nemesis of the materialist inversion of civilization, for the same common people, who welcomed the inception of civilization and were the main support of autocracy in the early phase of cultural development, now withdraw that support, and welcome the destruction of civilization in its materialist degeneration. A great change has come about in civilization since the early days, when nine-tenths of the surplus energy of the community were applied to the glorification of the Church or the State, that is to say, directly to the service of the superorganism itself, and the common people are not slow to realize the redirection of their energies. While they were willing and eager to take their part in the restoration of cultural ascendancy, and worked in the sweat of their brows to construct pyramids and cathedrals to the glory of the state, they are now no longer willing to grant this same service for the mere materialist gratification and piling-up of wealth of a plutocratic minority, who have lost all interest and respect for culture for its own sake.

While a man will gladly sacrifice his life for his religion or his country, he will not willingly sacrifice it to make a wealthy millionaire still wealthier. As materialism has destroyed all real superorganic spirit in civilization, and the degeneration of religion shows the decline of that intrinsic spirit, there is nothing left to which the human individual may sacrifice himself or offer his service. It is quite in vain that the plutocracy offers its doles of luxury and amusement, as that loyalty which is not freely rendered cannot be bought. The proletariat is embittered, and has lost all respect or liking for a government which after promising equality condemns the many to become the slaves of the wealth of the few. It does not matter if the proletariat of the democratic phase is considerably better off than the original subjects of autocracy, and has all the benefits of a vast industrial organization built up to suppply its wants, the superorganic reality of civilization is dead, and there is no higher cause which has the prestige to command the loyalties of the people. Civilization may and does stagger on for a time against ever-increasing difficulties under the guidance of plutocracy, but the common people have withdrawn their support.

The plutocratic leaders of the democratic state are compelled to purchase support and co-operation from the surrounding barbarians to maintain the functions of civilization, and these gradually encroach upon and finally destroy the material structure of the state, when the accumulated wealth of the plutocracy no longer suffices to appease the voracity of their greed. Nothing is more remarkable in the final collapse of civilization before barbarian invasion than the apathy with which the proletariat regards the destruction of the state. The same people, who in the earlier nationalist phase sacrificed themselves in thousands and millions to the short-sighted patriotism of their day, do not lift a finger, although it is now no question of which national state shall be supreme in civilization, but of the existence of civilization itself. If further evidence were required of the fact that civilization has become a burden to the greater part of the community, this lack of all patriotic response to the danger of extinction would supply it in a most decisive manner. The barbarians are welcomed by a proletariat only too glad to lose its chains, and civilization expires unwept and unsung.

THE SOCIAL CYCLE

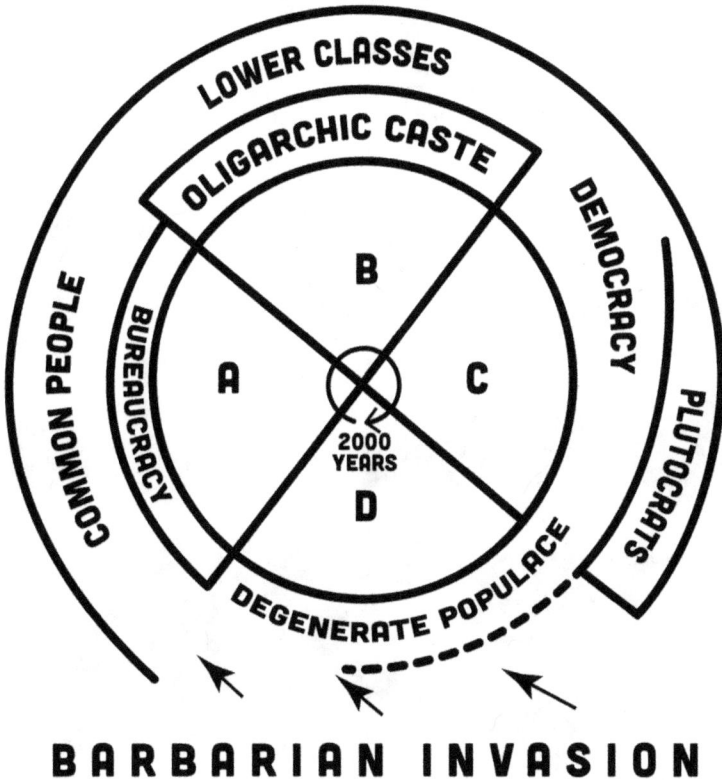

BARBARIAN INVASION

This cycle differs very considerably from the two foregoing, as it possesses a much greater continuity of development. The impetus to the whole social and cultural system is obviously given by the barbarian invasion in quadrant D, which introduces fresh virile blood to mingle with that of the civilized populace worn out in the preceding cycle. The bureaucratic and oligarchic sections of the community direct the evolution of civilization in its primitive forms, until in quadrant C the whole social community is enabled to enjoy for a time the fruits of civilized co-operation, until the usurpation of power by plutocracy. We may assume a 'nadir' at the time of barbarian invasion, although this is the time when the community is rejuvenated from the reservoir of primitive society, but here again the 'zenith' is a matter of opinion.

Chapter 6

The Language Cycle

When the first original civilizations arose the language of their peoples was naturally that of the barbarian stock, which first adopted agriculture. Several such original civilized languages are known, although some have been entirely lost. We have the early Coptic of Ancient Egypt: the Sumerian of the first practically unknown Mesopotamian civilization: the Dravidian of the equally unknown civilization of India prior to the Aryan invasion: ancient Chinese: as the original civilized tongues of the Old World. Where nomadic invasion does not introduce a large element of barbarian population into the civilized domain, the original language may remain the tongue of the government and of the people through long eras of culture. It was, however, only in the narrow, circumscribed valley of the Nile that such conditions of lingual continuity were fulfilled.

In Egypt, the short-lived invasion of the Hyksos left little, if any, racial effects upon the Egyptian people, and there are certainly no Semitic influences to be traced in the ancient Egyptian language. This continuity of language and of script had undoubtedly a very strong effect in producing the conservatism of Egyptian forms and the final 'Renaissance' of the primitive school of art at Memphis in the last 'Dammerung' of Egyptian culture.

When civilization wanes, nomadic invasion brings final destruction and nomad immigration in pursuit of the loot and rapine of decadent democracy. This immigration is in many cases on such a scale that a permanent barbarian element is introduced into the civilized region, which brings its own language with it to become the popular speech of the next cultural epoch. Varying degrees of coalescence with the existing language of the former democratic community may produce varying dialects depending upon the percentage of barbarians and original population in the different districts of the former civilized domain, but wherever an appreciable barbarian element is introduced into the civilized community a new form of popular speech will be developed. The gradual process of nomadic infiltration into the civilizations of the Old World from the northern steppes and the resultant modifications of language may be traced as follows:—

141

Civilization As Divine Superman

On the northern steppes of Europe and Asia at the inception of civilization in the more southerly desert belt there were three great nomadic groups of peoples, each with its own generic language: the Aryans in the west; the Semites in the centre about the Caspian Sea; the Turanians in the east. When the earliest Sumerian civilization in Mesopotamia collapsed, a part of the Semites moved south and invaded Mesopotamia in search of the plunder of the cities of the plains. They introduced their Semitic form of speech, which eventually coalesced with Sumerian to form the hybrid Babylonian. Then, on the simultaneous decline of both Babylonian and Egyptian civilizations, a further great Semitic irruption brought the Kassites to Babylon and the Hyksos to Egypt. The people of the Nile survived this attack practically unaffected, expelling the Hyksos to form the famous population of Palestine; but in Mesopotamia the last relics of Sumerian speech were submerged to give place to the popular Aramaic and Arabic of Mesopotamian civilization.

Meantime the Aryan nomadic group had spread eastwards to occupy the steppe lands abandoned by the Semitic group, which was now almost completely absorbed into civilization. Pressing south, they entered Persia, so that when the early Sudra civilization in India became decadent some time after 1000 B.C., it was the Aryans, and not the Semites, who invaded the valleys of the Indus and Ganges. They introduced their own language in singular purity as the basis of Hindu speech for the future. Further west, whatever the lost language of Minoa may have been, Aryan languages such as Greek and Latin came to the fore when civilization spread to the mainland of Europe. Finally, when Roman democracy standardized Mediterranean civilization, Latin became the language of the Mediterranean basin, while in the north the Teutonic language was the tongue of the remaining unabsorbed Aryan peoples. With the collapse of Rome, the Teutonic peoples moved southward to plunder the wealth of the Empire, and remained to coalesce with the Roman populace, forming the Romance languages of the present day. Thus we have in modern times in Europe a number of languages formed from the two sources of German and Latin in varying proportions as the barbarian or Latin element of the population predominated.

When the Aryans followed the Semites into civilization, the northern steppes, now somewhat restricted by the spread of civilization, were left almost entirely to the eastern Turanian group of nomadic peoples, known as Huns, Turks or Mongols. These moved westwards to occupy the Central Asian regions abandoned by the Semites and Aryans in turn as these found homes in the civilized south. When, later, both

The Language Cycle

Mesopotamian and Chinese civilizations were tottering to their fall, the Turanian peoples also migrated to the south, overwhelming Mesopotamia and China. A large element of barbarian blood was thus infused into the Chinese people, and the Turks settled in large numbers in the Levant. The Turanians did not reach India until a later period, and there failed to gain any real footing, leaving practically no trace in the Hindu language.

Thus we have three main periods of nomadic invasion of civilization and the immigration of barbarian stock, connected in each case with one of the original nomadic groups. First the Semites, then the Aryans, and lastly the Turanians have found their way into civilization, until today only a small part of the original Turanian family remains true to ancestral nomadic life on the Central Asian plains.

Although an intercultural barbarism generally leads to an immense immigration of barbarian peoples, and a complete change of popular speech, yet when civilization revives it must inevitably owe its origin to the remnant of culture from the former cultural era, and not to any intrinsic inspiration of some mystic order in the newly immigrated barbarian peoples. Civilization is super-racial; it is true to its cultural descent and not to any race of however superior quality. A descendant civilization is conceived by an earlier superorganism, if it is born with much pain and suffering of a barbarian people. Modern civilization owes its origin not to any excellence in the Teutonic race, as the Germans would have us believe, but to the inspiration of classical Roman culture working in the virgin ground of the barbarian Teutonic character.

As this is assuredly the case, it is not surprising to find that the early autocratic phase of civilization is remarkable for the dual nature of language. The common people as a whole speak the new popular tongue sprung from the coalescence of the barbarian language with the former speech of the civilized community, which will have many local dialects depending upon the several original tribes and their varying intermixture with the former populace. The bureaucratic administrators of autocracy, on the other hand, will speak the language of former civilization, which is the source of that superior culture, which entitles them to take the leading part in the restoration of civilization. We have thus a common form of speech, or variety of dialects, for vulgar intercourse between the people, and a distinct language of culture and literature learned and used exclusively by the bureaucracy in their position of cultural supremacy over the people. The bureaucratic use of the former language of civilization instead of the new barbarian dialects has a double advantage. In the first place, it enables the bureaucracy to maintain and strengthen its cultural supremacy by resource to the literature of the past era of civilization; and it gives in the second place the tremendous and imperative assistance to the administration of a great empire that despite local differences of speech and dialect all officials possess a common means of administrative intercourse.

In European civilization, the language of the foregoing Roman culture was the language of the Church, and hence of all learning, during the whole period of papal authority, all papal decrees being published in Latin text. Intercourse within the priesthood was invariably in Latin, so that priests drawn from England and Italy, Spain and Poland, might work together for the good of the Church. The monasteries, as centres of learning, promoted Latin from the speech of the clergy to the language of intercourse of all learning, while kings and statesmen used the same universal tongue as the language of medieval diplomacy.

It should not, however, be thought that this is an exceptional case of a language persisting through a Dark Age of barbarism to become the learned language of the future. The Mesopotamian series of civilizations gives a singularly perfect example of the repeated survival of the popular language of the foregoing era to become the learned language of administration in the succeeding cultural era.

Sumerian had a singular effect upon the language of the Semitic invaders who formed the succeeding Babylonian civilization. Even in the time of the democratic Babylonian Empire, Sumerian was largely the basis of the cuneiform writing, showing clearly that Sumerian must have survived for some time into Babylonian civilization in the form of literature and a source of learning.

After the further Semitic invasion of the Kassites, Babylonian became the language of culture and administration in Assyria used by the Assyrian scribes, despite the fact that the common people now spoke an entirely different Semitic dialect, known as Aramaic.

Early in Mesopotamian civilization, upon the fall of Assyria, Aryan invasion established the Persians within the bounds of the civilized domain, and the Persian language formed one of the two popular forms of speech in the Caliphate. It then survived to form the court language of the Sultanate in modern Levantine Civilization after the invasion and destruction of Turks and Mongols.

The Language Cycle

Even where the simple rule of the survival of the popular tongue of democracy to become the learned language of autocracy is not exactly fulfilled, we find that autocratic bureaucracy invariably adopts some definite dialect as the official language of state and administration. A common means of administrative intercourse is such an absolute necessity to an autocratic bureaucracy, that when it does not naturally arise out of the survival of learning from a former age it must be artificially devised by the state.

Thus we find in India, after the Aryan invasion, that the original Dravidian language of Sudra Civilization was entirely superseded by Aryan dialects in the north, while surviving in the south. When the Aryans came to restore civilization, they chose one of their own dialects, Pali, as the official language of administration. This choice was undoubtedly in large degree dictated by the fact that Buddha was held to have spoken in Pali, which was on that account the holy language of the Buddhist priests, who formed under Asoka the administration of his Empire.

A couple of thousand years later the Mogul Emperors restored Indian civilization after a period of anarchy, and found themselves faced with the same difficulty of organizing a united administration in face of the many languages and dialects of India. They solved the problem by adopting the Persian of the former Moslem regime in Delhi, and forced the peoples of India to learn this language in order to understand the official proclamations and other acts of autocratic administration. The Hindu people made a valiant effort, but only succeeded in producing the hybrid 'Hindustani,' half-Persian, half-native dialect, which has remained the official language of the Indian Empire ever since.

In China, after the expulsion of the Mongols, a number of different spoken dialects existed from north to south, depending upon the admixture of barbarian with native blood; but as the ancient ideographic script remained, however it might be pronounced, there was no need to study the ancient form of the Chinese language, still preserved in South China, in order to gain access to the legacy of past learning.

The Mandarin regime of the autocratic Ming emperors, however, found it necessary to advance the comparatively barbaric dialect of the neighbourhood of the capital, Pekin, to the standard of an official state language. This 'mandarin' language is indeed the classical Chinese of the present day.

Civilization As Divine Superman

When national disruption destroys the unity of the autocratic government of civilization, the state language of bureaucracy immediately suffers eclipse, largely on account of national enmity towards the former autocratic regime, and also because of rising local loyalties, which raise local dialects to the level of national languages. Then it is that the barbarian tongues come into their own. In the period of autocracy the language of past culture alone is considered worth perpetuation in the form of literature, and the common tongue of the people is regarded as too vulgar for the honour of becoming a vehicle of literary expression. With the extinction of the 'dead' language of a dead and gone cultural epoch of the past, however, the vulgar tongues of the people do, after all, become literary vehicles, and are found to be much more alive and vigorous than the musty language of the past. It is true that a great diversity of national tongues takes the place of the universal State language of autocracy, but this is quite in accordance with the political disruption of civilization, and the spirit of patriotism comes as an additional inspiration to local literary attainment.

In Europe, when Latin ceased to be the only cultivated language, an immense inspiration passed to the barbaric vulgar tongues of the Teutonic peoples, with their varying admixture of Roman elements. Italian, Spanish, French, English, German became at about the time of the Reformation national languages of high esteem instead of mere vulgar coarse popular jargon. All at once men of high literary ability began to write in their own native dialects instead of in the Church's Tatin Dante, Cervantes, Rabelais, Shakespeare produced triumphs of literature each in another national tongue, while Luther in Germany actually had the temerity to translate the Bible from the Holy Latin of the Church into the vulgar German of the common people.

In Mediterranean civilization, after the disruption of the Minoan autocracy, the various dialects of the barbarian Greeks became vehicles of the most wonderful literary accomplishment.

In India, the period of Raja disruption from early Buddhist autocratic administration led to the decline of Pali as the Holy Tongue of Buddha and the rise of the other dialects of the Aryan language along with the former Dravidian, to form the modern diversity of Indian

In modern times the collapse of the Sultanate has led to the revival of local dialects throughout the former Turkish Empire, and the decline of Persian and Arabic as the learned languages of the past. The Turks themselves, under the guidance of their national leader Kemal have

146

exalted their own Turanian language, and have actually divested it of the Arabic script, in which it had always formerly been written, to mark its freedom from Arabic and Persian leading strings.

When a civilization in the oligarchic phase falls to the conquest of a foreign race, either barbarian or from a neighbouring civilization, a foreign language is introduced, but the invading race under these circumstances forms an exclusive caste of conquerors, which lives in complete seclusion from the people as a whole, and their language remains shut off from the general lingual stock. When the caste of conquerors finally succumbs, little trace of their language remains in the native tongue owing to the lack of intermixture between the dominant caste and the people as a whole. It is, indeed, astonishing how little permanent effect of any kind such an imperialist epoch has upon later cultural development. Within comparatively few decades all trace of the intrusive foreign caste is lost, as if they had never been.

The Ethiopians, of entirely foreign negroid stock, invaded and conquered all Egypt under the auspices of Ammon. They remained for some time as a dominant military caste in Egypt, yet in later times no trace of their customs or speech was to be found in the culture of the Egyptian 'Renaissance' at Memphis.

The Greeks in the train of Alexander's armies settled throughout Mesopotamian civilization, and founded their city states in which they lived as a dominant military and commercial caste. For at least a couple of centuries they maintained their political ascendancy, and for a long time after losing this political power remained the highly esteemed commercial community of the Persian Empire. Yet there is nothing more remarkable in history than the eventual complete submergence of this Helenistic caste in the native population, so that no trace remained of its former domination. Not even a Greek word in the Persian or Aramaic languages survived as a remembrance of the great era of Hellenism. Manchu domination in China lasted for very nearly three hundred years, and only ceased less than twenty years ago, and yet at the present time Manchu influences are already practically extinct in China, and the Manchu language has certainly left no permanent trace in modern Chinese speech.

In India, British rule has introduced the English language as the speech of the dominant caste, yet there can be no doubt that English customs and the English language will not survive the eventual withdrawal of the British from India.

Democracy advances the ideal of social equality, and hence leads to a standardization of culture. One of the most important features of this standardization is the adoption of a standard language for general intercourse within the democratic empire. As the first nation to promote democratic revolution has conquered the other peoples, its speech has gained a high prestige, and is also the official language of administration and justice. Under the circumstances it is not surprising that the other peoples adopt this tongue as their own standard of mutual intercourse, although no compulsion is brought upon them to do so. The universal peace of democracy enables the several nations and races of the empire to enter into intimate commercial and social intercourse with one another, when one common speech becomes imperative. Just as the bureaucrats of early autocracy found that they could not administer a great empire without the aid of some means of administrative intercourse, so the emancipated common people of a later epoch find that they, too, must learn a common language of everyday speech if they are themselves to control and enjoy the fruits of democratic empire.

Actually this standardization of language is only one symptom of a general intermixture of race, which is typical of democratic empire. Universal peace and the abolition of national boundaries, combined with the emancipation of the common people from the restrictions and burdens of serfdom, lead to a general interchange of peoples between all parts of the democratic empire, so that all national and even racial divisions become blurred and indistinct within a few generations. After a century or two of such unprecedented free movement of population, it is no longer possible to make any clear distinction between the people of one part of the empire and those of any other, and one speaks instinctively of all the people by one generic name, as if some new race were come into existence, as it indeed has. All the people of civilization have become stirred up into one great conglomerate, within which are all the elements of the original civilized race, and such barbarian migrations as have revitalized civilization in the past. This conglomerate is, in fact, actually a new democratic race.

Babylonia is the first great democratic empire of which we have reliable record, and although Babylon was originally only an obscure city among many others on the Mesopotamian plains, yet it was Babylon that gave the name to the Babylonian Empire, the Babylonian people, and the Babylonian language. For many centuries Babylonia and Mesopotamia were synonymous terms, just as at a later date the Roman Empire and the basin of the Mediterranean were synonymous. Clearly only a great process of standardization, both racial and lingual, could have brought this centralization upon the culture and speech of one city on a whole people.

In modern times we have seen how the great democratizing conquests of Napoleon spread the French language as a vehicle of revolutionary administration and justice deep into Central Europe, and there can be little doubt that had Napoleon's Empire been sustained, French would have become the standard administrative, and eventually popular, language of all Europe.

In America the huge immigrant population, which already largely outnumbers the original Anglo-Saxon colonial stock and still possesses a higher birth-rate, does not retain the home tongue of its diverse European origin, but adopts (and distorts) the English of the original settlers. Not only is a distinct race, the American, being produced from the conglomeration of European national and racial stocks, but a distinct language, the American, is being developed by the adaptation of English to the intercourse of American democracy.

In some cases the process of standardization may be only partially realized owing to the existence of some other language of high repute from the earlier oligarchic epoch. We may have in such a case a dual standardization in which one half of the empire uses the language of democratic revolution, while the other half remains faithful to the older speech of oligarchy. At first revolutionary prestige will invest the democratic tongue with the superior place as the official language of government, but in course of time the older form of speech may prevail.

There are two great examples of this duality in democratic speech. The Roman Empire spoke predominantly Latin, as the official language of the imperial administration, but in the Levant Greek remained the speech of the people and of commerce. When the western part of the Empire was submerged by barbarian invasion, the remaining Eastern Empire soon reverted to Greek as its official language of government. This lingual cleavage had, and still has, an important result in later times, as the western European nations gained their culture through Latin sources, while the eastern nations drew theirs from Greek. This double source of culture has given rise not only to the Roman and Greek Churches and a Roman and Greek script, but to an essential cleavage of European civilization, which is still a barrier to European reunion. Napoleon himself came to grief on his failure to appreciate this fundamental difference of Russian from Western culture, when he endeavoured to extend his imperial control over foreign Russia.

In the Caliphate, a very similar process brought an identical duality of language and culture, when Arabic played the role of Latin and Persian that of Greek. Until the fall of the Omayyad Caliphate, Arabic was the one and only language of Islam. With the revolt of Persia, and the inauguration of the Abassids as Caliphs in place of the Omayyads, the language of the foregoing oligarchy returned into its own, and Persian became the standard language of the eastern part of the vast Caliphate domains, while Arabic remained the speech of the west. This duplication of language had a similar, and even more far-reaching, effect upon the future of the Near East, when Arabic had a strong effect upon the rejuvenation of Levantine civilization, and Persian passed with the invading Moslems to India, where it became the language of the Moslem regime at Delhi, and eventually formed the basis of the Hindustani of the Mogul administration.

THE LANGUAGE CYCLE

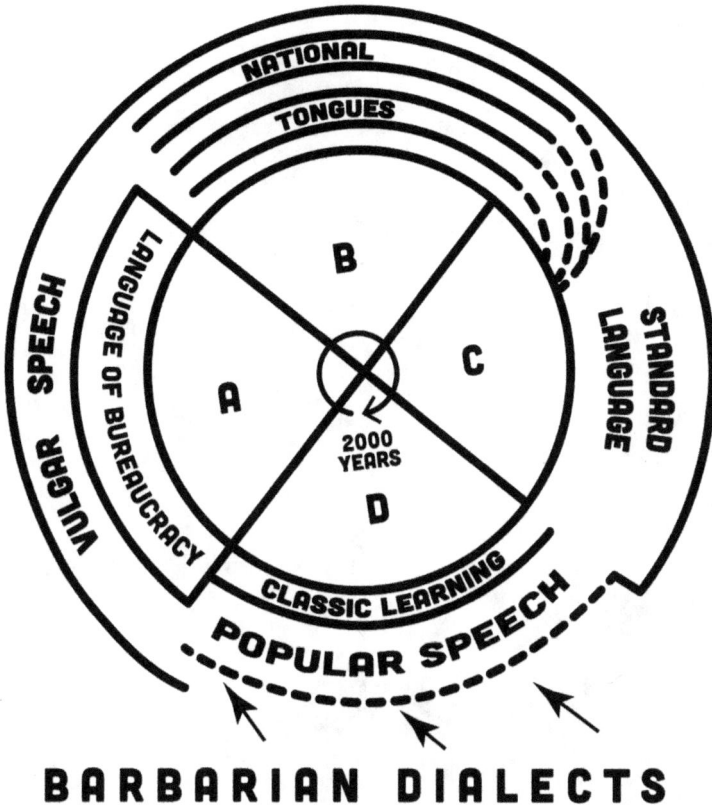

The form of this cycle is very similar to the foregoing social cycle, depending as it does upon racial influences. A distinct feature is, however, to be seen in the survival of the standard language of democracy through the period of barbarian invasion to become the official language of autocratic bureaucracy on the restoration of civilization. Here, for the first time, we find a definite continuity across quadrant D, so that this quadrant does not function so clearly as a break in cultural unity, as it does in the political and economic cycles. The cycle has indeed adopted the form of a re-entering spiral, and symbolizes the vortex of civilization absorbing primitive races, and using their virile energies for the furtherance of its superorganic aims. Here it is impossible to speak of either 'nadir' or 'zenith.'

Chapter 7

The Religious Cycle

True religion in the form of a feeling of universal brotherhood in God and a higher destiny behind human affairs is completely denied to primitive society. The savage seems overburdened with religious beliefs and observances, but a little examination of them reveals their superstitious nature. He does not revere one supreme God in return for His aid and protection; on the contrary he recognizes the existence of a whole pantheon of gods and goddesses, some benevolent, but more malevolent, who must all be propitiated to gain their favour and avoid their evil powers. It is quite clear that each of these deities personifies some natural object or natural force, which primitive man has learned to respect and fear. There are gods and goddesses of sun and moon, thunder and lightning, winds and rivers, mountains and seas, volcanoes and earthquakes, not to speak of the common human passions, such as love and hate, war and peace. Every natural phenomenon, which is too vast or too mysterious for the understanding of the primitive individual mind, is imbued with 'religious' significance. Owing to the inevitably subjective nature of primitive thought it is only natural that the savage projects human attributes upon the natural phenomena about him, and personifies them in the form of gods and goddesses with human, all too human, propensities. All primitive peoples have built up similar pantheons from their subjective reactions to the world of nature about them, but those of the Aryans are perhaps the best developed of all.

The Roman and Greek mythology includes typical examples of natural personifications: Apollo, god of the sun; Jupiter, wielder of the thunderbolt ; Vulcan, god of volcanoes; and many others.

The Teutonic gods and goddesses are similarly allied to natural forces, although differing in many particulars from the deities of the classical mythology of the south. Thor, god of thunder, and Loki, god of the lightning, are typical examples.

As true religion is denied to primitive society, we should expect to find the first beginnings of true religious belief upon the original foundation of civilization at the dawn of history. There are five cases of early civilizations, which are known to historical record, and yet do not seem to have been preceded by any still earlier cultural system in the same region. These five civilizations are Mediterranean, Early Egyptian, Early Chinese, Japanese, and Peruvian. The first autocratic phases of these civilizations were centred upon the Minos rulers of Knossus, the early Pharaohs at Memphis, the Shang and Chou Emperors in China, the early Mikados in Japan, the Incas at Cusco. One significant bond unites all these early autocratic regimes, a state religion centred upon the autocratic ruler himself as the representative of a new supreme God upon earth.

Although we know little of Minoan civilization, Greek legend points to the deification of the king, Minos, who claimed a yearly tribute of youths and maidens as slaves to his vast metropolis, Knossus, on Crete. The priestly office of the Minoan kings has only recently been confirmed by excavation revealing the very temples of the Minoan cult.

In Egypt, the early Pharaohs were associated with the great creative god, Re, from whom they were assumed to be descended through the gods of civilizing influences, Osiris and Horus. Indeed, the name Horus as indicative of divine descent remained associated with the office of Pharaoh throughout Egyptian history. The veneration of the Egyptian people for the Pharaohs of the early dynasties is amply shown by the immense pyramids they erected to their memory, monuments which have remained unsurpassed in sheer bulk and grandeur to the present day.

In early China, similarly, the first semi-legendary emperors were conceived as being the descendants of the gods, through certain semi-divine civilizing beings. The creative element was known as T'ien, a sort of impersonal heaven to be compared with the Nirvana of the Buddhists, while with T'ien was associated Shang-Ti, the supreme ruler. The emperors all bore the title T'ien-Tzi, or son of heaven, and possessed in early times the monopoly of the priestly office.

In Japan, according to the Shinto religion, the work of creation was accomplished by a spiritual dual, Izanagi, the male principal, and Izanani, the female principal, from whom through Amaterasu, the goddess of the sun, and Jimmu, the first emperor, all the Mikados have been descended in an unbroken line down to the present day. It is a well-known fact that the Mikado enjoys even today the veneration of his subjects as a semi-divine personage.

In ancient Peru the Incas were held to be descended directly from Manco Capac and Mama Oello, who brought civilization to Peru.

Manco was known as the 'Son of the Sun,' and enjoyed the direct veneration of his subjects, as did all his descendants. Indeed, it was the extreme veneration of the person of the Inca that made it possible for Pizarro to rule in his name and consolidate the conquest of his empire after he had taken Atahualpa, the thirteenth Inca, prisoner.

As we see, it is the autocratic ruler, the founder of civilization, who takes the place of the animistic pantheon in primitive religious belief, and enjoys the direct veneration of his subjects. The advent of civilization has in large measure deprived the forces of nature of their former terrors, and has endowed civilized man with a new understanding of the objective reality of the world about him. The gods and goddesses of primitive superstition inevitably lose their potency in the more enlightened era of civilization, and the newly civilized community turns its worship from them to the autocratic founder of this new cultural system. Civilization has indeed become a phenomenon vaster and more mysterious than any of the phenomena of nature, that had formerly awakened the awe of primitive man. Sheltered within the bounds of this new great super-organism, civilized man no longer fears the forces of nature; on the contrary, he joins with his comrades in the subjugation of nature, taming unruly rivers despite their floods, irrigating deserts in the face of the cruel blazing sun, launching sailing ships to use the stormy winds, even turning the tides to his service. How can he retain any respect for the gods and goddesses of natural forces, when they have thus become the slaves of his newly found civilization? But on the other hand, how great must his respect for civilization become, and with what awe must he approach the autocratic ruler who has made all this possible? It is no wonder that the first great autocrats of civilization have trod the ground as demigods revered by their grateful peoples, and have been immortalized by monuments and mausoleums, which awaken the awe and admiration even of our day.

Yet, despite this deification of their autocratic leaders, the first cultural communities still realize that the great ruler in their midst with all his magnificence and glory is after all a mortal man of like stature with themselves. They appreciate in some measure that he merely represents in his person the great superorganic system that has grown up about him, through the united efforts of generations of his forefathers and their ministers. In every state-religion of these early times we find the vast shadow of a supreme God hovering above and behind the mortal autocrat, who professes to represent this supreme Deity on earth, and be guided by His instructions. Usually this God has advanced from among the old primitive pantheon (where He has generally played the role of god of the sun), but as the other animistic deities decline, this one advances to reign supreme in the veneration of the civilized community, losing by degrees all special association with the sun or any other natural phenomenon in a general omnipotence. As the earlier pantheon was formed by the personification of the various natural forces, to which primitive man was subjected, this new supreme God must, according to the same argument, be the personification of some new super-natural power, which awakens the awe and mystification of civilized man. There is only one such supernatural power, which has come into existence with the beginning of cultural co-operation. This is the superorganism, civilization, which is already displaying supernatural powers, subjugating nature to its superorganic ends. The first great God of civilization represents thus the superorganic spirit of civilization dimly apprehended by the human members of the new super being; and the semi-divine autocrat, who directs the administration of the state, is the representative of this divine superman upon earth.

Although the gods and goddesses of the original primitive pantheon are during the epoch of autocracy completely overshadowed by the supreme God chosen by the civilized community to represent the superorganic spirit of civilization, yet their memory is not completely lost, and upon the decline of autocratic empire they frequently return into their own in a new form. The centralized authority of autocracy becomes, as we have seen, intolerable to the peoples subjected to it, and eventually a violent disruption rends the fabric of autocratic empire, producing from it a number of independent national states. It is inevitable that this sudden disruption of superorganic unity should be accompanied by a similar disruption of the unity of the godhead of the civilized community. Autocratic empire no longer exists, hence the monotheistic godhead as an expression of the collective soul of that empire must also cease to exist. New national states have come into being, and new national gods must be conceived to represent these new collective but minor souls into which the former united soul of civilization has been disrupted. Where an original religion has been centred upon the person of the autocrat himself, it is obvious that the passing of autocratic authority must have the inevitable effect of extinguishing the worship of the personal ruler as the representative of God upon earth. In most cases of this kind the autocrat has been associated with the supreme god of a tribal pantheon, that has survived from the earlier state of barbarism, and the passing of autocratic authority is the signal for the resuscitation of those gods and goddesses, which were for a time overshadowed by His name. The revolting states not only renounce the authority of the autocratic regime, but abandon the state religion, which was such a strong support to this government. Each adopts one or another of the original tribal gods as its own private divinity, and a form of apparent polytheism in civilization is produced from a number of separate local monotheistic gods. Each local state, however, while serving its own god alone, is forced from considerations of foreign policy to accept the existence and formal equality of the gods of other states, even accepting the local authority of these gods on their own territory.

Thus Jehovah, as god of the ancient Jews, was only one of a number of local gods in Syria and Palestine, who arose with the growth of national consciousness after the withdrawal of the Egyptians on the collapse of the autocratic power of Thebes. There is plenty of evidence in the Old Testament that the Jews recognized the gods of their neighbours as powerful supernatural powers within the borders of the states where they were worshipped. It is only our intimate knowledge of the Jews through our study of their Bible that makes us think of them as monotheistic, as to a contemporary Assyrian Jehovah must have appeared as only one of a number of local gods among the polytheistic Syrian peoples.

In Egypt, at a much earlier date, after the decline of the early autocracy of Memphis, a number of local Egyptian cities made themselves independent, and each chose one or another of the primitive pantheon as their own local divinity. It was at this time that Thebes chose Ammon as its god, and determined the future ascendancy of the worship of Ammon in all Egypt, when Egyptian unity was restored by the princes of Thebes.

In Central America, at the time of the invasion of the Spaniards, a similar polytheism existed, each Maya and Aztec city having its local divinity in the general pantheon.

The Greeks, who invaded the Ægean region after the decline of Minoa, brought their own tribal divinities into Mediterranean civilization, and, for example, Athena was the goddess of Athens and Diana of Ephesus, while each city state worshipped one or other of the Greek pantheon, as the guardian divinity of the city.

Still more remarkable was the revival of the Vedic gods and goddesses of the Aryan invaders of India after the decline of Buddhism as the state religion of the Maurya empire. Brahmanism was based upon these primitive tribal deities, and has survived down to the present time. During the Raja disruption, which was the political condition of India from the decline of autocracy to the invasion of the Moslems, each separate state, and indeed most of the towns and villages of India worshipped one or other of the Brahmanic pantheon as their own guardian spirit.

So far we have found that the religious faith of early original and offshoot civilizations, deeply influenced as it was by primitive animism, has failed to produce any of the great religions of history.

These belong to a later period in cultural development, and are all associated with descendant civilizations. We find, however, that although these great religions can generally be shown to be geographically identical with the descendant cultural systems, of which they express the superorganic spirit, chronological identification is much less clearly marked. Indeed, a very strong criticism of the association of religion with the superorganic soul of civilization might be advanced on account of this failure of chronological parallelism. The great religions are definitely out of step with the rhythm of cultural development as shown by the political cycle. For example, the religion of Ammon was conceived in the later stages of Early Egyptian, but reached its height of temporal authority in the Late Egyptian cultural era: Christianity was taught by Jesus and diffused by Paul in the Roman democratic phase of Mediterranean civilization, but attained the full authority of autocratic government in the time of the Papacy in the European era: Islam was preached by Mahomet in the last phase of Mesopotamian civilization, yet played a very large part in the authoritative administration of the Sultanate in modern Levantine civilization. In general, however, although the great religions are not chronologically identical with the great cultural epochs, they are all uniformly 'out of step.' They take their origin in the waning phases of a foregoing civilization, survive the period of intercultural barbarism, inspire a following civilization, and reach a height of authority in this new cultural era. As the following civilization itself wanes, the extant religion is also in turn supplanted by a new and more virile faith.

Owing to the great authority gained by religion during the autocratic phase, there is a tendency to associate religions with the following rather than the foregoing civilization. Ammon is essentially the religion of Late Egyptian civilization after the Hyksos invasion: Buddhism the religion of India after the advent of the Aryans: Christianity attained Papal power after the barbarians had crushed the Roman Empire and a new European civilization was in being: even Islam enjoyed a more despotic authority under the Sultanate than in the materialist regime of the Caliphate. This association is no doubt perfectly justified, and if we apply it to the proposition of the identity of religion with the collective soul of civilization, we come to the interesting conclusion that the soul of the forthcoming civilization is conceived before the parent superorganism has become materially extinct. The still unborn superorganic civilization of the future is foreshadowed: its soul makes its presence felt in the waning materialist structure of extant civilization, although it is as yet denied a separate corporate existence.

The elder superorganism has already lost its soul in the craving for materialist gratification that imbues its human units. The democratic materialism of the last stages of civilization is atheistic and irreligious, because the human beings that make up civilization have denied the super-organic reality of their culture, and insist that civilization shall serve them instead of humbly serving the super-organic ends of civilization. They have, indeed, in very truth denied their God. Here we have the explanation of the Paganism of the Roman Empire: the gross material frivolity of the Caliphate: the modern neglect of religion. The democrat, when he denies all superior political authority, all higher cultural ability, exalts the individual at the expense of the collective superorganism, and clearly denies the superman any personal organic reality as distinct from the individuals of which he is composed. Under these circumstances it is not surprising that religion, which is the 'unconscious' appreciation of the presence of the divine superman, should suffer an eclipse.

Into this irreligious epoch a new religion is suddenly projected, which is highly critical of materialist preoccupations, and recalls mankind to a higher destiny. In this early stage all great religions are exceedingly virile, opposing a fierce hostility to material wealth and power, and directing popular attention to spiritual non-material enterprises to the neglect of worldly prosperity. Thus we find in the higher spiritual teaching of all great religions this same exaltation of non-material over material, of spiritual over worldly, which was developed in its first purity in the early reaction against triumphant materialism.

As the elder civilization is already waning, has already relapsed into materialist degeneration, the new religion expressing a revived belief in a higher destiny in man cannot be directed to the resuscitation of extant civilization. On the contrary it is directed to the destruction of the existing superorganism, which has already lapsed into senility. The ground must be cleared for the coming of the new civilization of the future, and the foreshadowing religion is directed primarily to the eradication of that materialism, which is the sole remaining feature of declining extant civilization. The hostility of religion to the social order is at its greatest in the early inception of the Church: at that time the future is at battle with the past, the unborn culture of future civilization is striving for an opportunity to develop its personality, and the senile parent must make place for its more vigorous descendant.

A further proof that the new religion cannot express an unconscious appreciation of the presence of the elder civilization, but is a foreshadowing of the civilization to come, is given by the fact that, when the elder civilization suffers complete extinction by barbarian invasion, the new religion still survives in the ruins of the past, and indeed gains a higher spiritual value by the elimination of plutocratic influences, which may have corrupted its first purity.

With the advent of a new civilization from the chaos of intercultural barbarism, religion comes into its own. It is no longer in conflict with existing social organization, but fully at amity with early cultural society. The super-organic civilization of which it is the soul has at last come into actual corporate existence: there is now no longer any question of a destructive anti-social policy: religion may at last enter actively into the organization and administration of the new state. Whereas in the democratic phase religion and the social order were at fierce enmity one with the other, in the autocratic phase of the following civilization they advance hand in hand; indeed religion and the social order are but two aspects of the same super-organic reality. At no time does religion reach such a height of authority as during the autocracy of descendant civilization. Then as at no other period of civilization is the unconscious instinct of superorganic existence made conscious by a despotic authority, which directs the collective energies at will. God and His people, the superman and his constituent human units, are in very close communion.

The existence of a powerful religious organization in descendant autocracy leads, however, to a dangerous condition of rivalry for supreme authority in those civilizations where the spiritual and temporal governments of the state are not united under one ruler. Happy the autocracy, like the Sultanate, that has united temporal and spiritual power under one omnipotent autocrat. In other civilizations two separate forms of service to superorganic reality exist: the one a conscious effort of government by the temporal ruler; the other an unconscious form of worship directed towards the image of the divine superman in the mirror of belief and controlled by the spiritual ruler. In a state of autocracy these two forms of service towards civilization may run approximately parallel, but perfect harmony may not always ensue, and there is always a strong temptation to bring both under one dominant control. Hence we find in almost every descendant autocracy in history a struggle between the state and the church, which may be decided in favour of either or neither, and in which the balance of power may rest now on one side and now on the other. Pharaoh and High Priest of Ammon: Assyrian King and Priest of Marduk at Babylon: Emperor and Pope: their mutual enmity is only equalled by their mutual need of one another.

Ammon

The Religion of Egyptian Civilization

The great religion of Egypt was that of Ammon. This god was originally the local god of Thebes following the disruption of the empire of Memphis, and gained a position of ascendancy when the Pharaohs of the XII dynasty made Thebes the capital of a reunited Egyptian Empire. The Hyksos invasion, which destroyed Early Egyptian civilization, was inimical to Ammon, as the Hyksos endeavoured to impose the worship of their own Syrian gods upon the Egyptians; but Ammon survived to be restored to the first place in Egyptian religion upon the expulsion of the Hyksos by the powerful XVIII dynasty. The great Pharaohs of the time endowed the vast temple at Karnak with immense riches, and the priesthood of Ammon rose to a position of the utmost prestige in Egypt. The conscious support of superorganic action by the direct temporal authority of the state was accompanied and rivalled by the unconscious support of the superorganism on the part of the priesthood, until the two forms of service became so nearly akin that a great struggle for joint mastery ensued. First of all the heretic, Akhenaton, sought to break the spiritual power of Ammon by favouring one of the other gods of the Egyptian pantheon, Aton, at his expense. This deliberate heresy, amounting as it did to a deliberate denial of the soul of Egypt, was doomed to failure and scarcely outlived its author, whose unfortunate nephew, Tutankhamen, was compelled to recant. Despite all recantation, the XVIII dynasty was overthrown, and a new dynasty friendly to Ammon installed in its place. This triumph of the Priesthood of Ammon over the authority of the Pharaohs established the high-priest in a position of complete dominion over the throne, and it was finally the high-priest Hrihor who deposed the last Theban Pharaoh and ruled alone. With the passing of the Pharaohs, however, Egypt immediately relapsed into a state of political disruption. The conscious and unconscious elements of cultural service has committed mutual homicide, and it is scarcely necessary to trace the later demoralization of Ammon that led to the unholy alliance with the Ethiopians and the foreign conquest of Egypt.

Marduk

The Religion Of Mesopotamian Civilization

The god Marduk, in Mesopotamia, plays very much the same role as Ammon in Egypt. There also Marduk, the local god of Babylon, rose to supreme importance with the authority of the Babylonian Empire, and survived the humiliation of Babylon in the barbarian invasion of the Kassites. With the restoration of civilization and Mesopotamian Empire by Assyrian autocrats, Marduk continued to hold first place among the gods of the Mesopotamian plain, and even the great Assyrian kings did not feel assured of imperial authority until they had paid their homage in the temple of Marduk at Babylon. Assyrian despotism was, however, of a very virile nature, and there was no tendency of the priesthood of Marduk to gain a position of supremacy over the state as in Egypt; but, nevertheless, it is significant that after the fall of Nineveh to the Medes and Persians the holy city of Babylon regained its old position of capital of the Mesopotamian Empire. Marduk represented the collective soul of Mesopotamian civilization, and even the tyrannical Assyrians did not dare offend so august a deity. It was only with the advent of the foreign culture of Hellenism that the Babylonian religion of Marduk came to an end.

Buddha

The Religion of Aryan civilization

The next religion in point of time, Buddhism, came nearer to a clear spiritual recognition of superorganic existence than any other religion either before or since. Buddha upheld the ideal of an impersonal, all-embracing spirit as his conception of the godhead, a spirit in which all human beings might submerge their individuality. Indeed, Buddha suggested the ultimate submergence of the petty, individual souls of men in the great collective soul of God as the last blissful reward of human perfection: that is the essence of Nirvana. There can be little doubt that Buddhism found its origin in that previous materialist civilization on the Indian plains that succumbed to Aryan invasion, for we find as the essential doctrine of Buddhism a violent revulsion against materialism, as the merest illusion, to the service of the spirit. Buddha taught the materialist-blinded people of his time the futility and mean wickedness of their craving after material wealth and sensual pleasure, showing them how materialistic preoccupations kept them earth-bound and denied them all higher spiritual perception.

After its inception in decadent Sudra civilization, Buddhism was for a time submerged in the veneration of the Aryan invaders towards their barbaric tribal gods; but with the advent of a new Indian civilization, in which the virile Aryans took the leading part, Buddhism came, nevertheless, into its own as an expression of the soul of the superorganism. The great emperor, Asoka, adopted Buddhism as the state religion of all India, and used the priesthood of Buddha as a form of bureaucratic administration of his vast imperial domains. Eventually, however, under the descendants of Asoka, the inevitable conflict between the state and the priesthood arose, and in India the struggle was finally decided in favour of the secular power. Buddhism declined to be replaced once more by the tribal gods of the Brahmanic pantheon.

Buddhism was not, however, on that account extinguished as a great religious force, but passed to the offshoot civilizations of Indian inspiration in Ceylon, Java and Burma, in the first and last of which regions it has survived to the present day. It passed also by way of Central Asia to China and Japan, in which it has had the most powerful effect upon the development of indigenous religious faith, combining with Taoism in China and Shintoism in Japan to form hybrid faiths of considerable merit. Indeed, Buddhism has proved the most powerful religious ideal in history, and despite the passing of Aryan civilization in India, still remains, on account of its great value as a spiritual recognition of the nature of superorganic reality a powerful element in Oriental thought and philosophy to this day.

J Christ

The Religion of European Civilization

The resemblance between the gospel of Jesus Christ and the teaching of Buddha is quite remarkable. Christianity and Buddhism are perhaps the highest expression of the religious instinct in man, and were both conceived in violent revulsion against effete materialism. Jesus called again and again upon the people of Palestine to turn their attention from corruptible wealth to the incorruptible things of the spirit, to give no thought to the personal needs of the morrow, but to rely upon the paternal protection of God. Although Jesus did not approach to the philosophical conception of God as an impersonal, all-pervading spirit, as did Buddha, yet he also thought of God as being in all men and all men as being of God. When Jesus suffered death at the hands of the local god of the Jews, the great missionary Paul carried the new teaching to the slave population of the Roman Empire, already groaning under the load of materialist plutocracy. Christianity rose by degrees from the lowest classes of the community to become the state religion of the Roman Empire, but only after triumphantly sustaining cruel persecution at the hands of the state. In fact, Christianity was to the last essentially antagonistic to the whole materialist social order of the Roman Empire, and hence passed quite naturally to the barbarian hordes, which finally conquered Rome. Indeed, when European civilization arose from the wreckage of inter-cultural barbarism, the Christian Church was already so powerful that it soon wrested temporal power from the Frankish Emperors and decided the conflict of State and Church by ruling alone. The Pope, as the head of the Catholic Church, became the autocrat of Christendom, and in very truth the representative of God upon earth. Yet the Catholic Church was to suffer from the usurpation of temporal power, despite the logical unity of control which it gained, for when in the fullness of time the local rulers and their peoples became impatient of the political centralization of the Papacy as an imperial autocracy, they found themselves compelled to renounce the spiritual authority of the Church along with its temporal authority, as the two had become so inextricably interwoven. Thus, although the main object of the Reformation was the liberation of local temporal rulers from Papal domination (see Henry VIII), the most spectacular result was the spiritual reaction from the Catholic Church by the people of Northern Europe. Although Christianity survived the Reformation, it was forced in all the states of Europe to take a secondary place once more in relation to the newly restored national authorities, and even compelled within our own lifetime to prostitute Christian doctrines to the support of nationalist patriotisms in the blood-bath of world war.

TAO

THE RELIGION OF CHINESE CIVILIZATION

In the early classical age of Chinese culture the philosopher Lau Tzi produced a highly idealistic ethical system professing a great contempt for all active individual effort by mankind. His most important saying was, 'Do nothing, and all things will be done,' which bears a striking resemblance in a philosophic form to Jesus's advice to 'Take no thought for the morrow, for the morrow will take thought for itself.' Both these sayings would be pure insanity if some higher being were not conceived as being occupied in ordering human affairs. Hence Lau Tzi was the prophet of a new religion, which his followers termed

'Tao,' the Way of Salvation. At first little more than a philosophic idea, Taoism was developed during the succeeding centuries into a true religious belief in a supreme God to whose communion human beings might ascend when they had learned to put worldly things and futile material activities from them. In fact, in its later development Taoism approached very closely to the form already adopted by Buddhism, and when the older religion reached China from India the two anti-materialist ideals gravitated together and formed a growing protest against the materialism and self-indulgence of waning Early Chinese civilization. In the time of the Tang and Sung dynasties, Taoism and Buddhism had advanced to a power in the state, and were persecuted by the Chinese Emperors just as was Christianity by the Roman Emperors. The Mongol invasion, when it eventually came to destroy Early Chinese culture, was not antagonistic to the Buddhist and Taoist faiths, the Mongols themselves being primitive Buddhists; and after the expulsion of the Mongols by the Ming Emperors these two religions completed their conversion of the Chinese peoples. Possibly owing to the dual nature of Chinese religious faith, neither Buddhism nor Taoism attained any great temporal power in the state, and the traditional conflict of spiritual and temporal authority did not arise to disturb Chinese political tranquillity. As religion was not confused with imperial government, both Buddhism and Taoism survived the fall of the Ming unimpaired, and persisted through the Confucian regime of the Manchus to take pride of first place in Chinese religious and philosophic life to this day.

ISLAM

THE RELIGION OF LEVANTINE CIVILIZATION

Although Islam is a degraded form of religion as compared with Buddhism, Christianity, or even Taoism, it must yet be granted a place as a monotheistic world religion. Mahomet was no great philosopher, like Buddha or Lau Tzi, or a moral genius like Jesus; -he was a mere rebel priest driven by the hostility of his own town, Mecca, into active opposition to the existent order of society. As the time was ripe for social revolution in Mesopotamian civilization, Mahomet became the centre of a great social movement, which he neither understood nor made any pretension to control. With this unpromising source, Islam was too easily deflected to a mere cloak for materialist democracy, and it was left for later reformers to supply the lacking higher spiritual essence, without which no religion can possibly survive. Hence we find the history of Islam disturbed by innumerable 'Reformations,' and violent protests by Carmathians and Assassins against the degenerate plutocratic tendencies of the later Caliphate. It is no doubt to these spiritual revulsions against Caliphate materialism that Islam owed its survival through Mongol destruction to become the administrative inspiration of the Turkish Sultanate. In the Sultanate we have an instance of the opposite result of the tendency towards unity of spiritual and temporal authority from that which took place in the Papacy, as here the temporal authority of the Turkish Sultan and the spiritual authority of the Caliph were united in the hands of the former, who bore both titles simultaneously. Exactly as in Papal Europe, the Sultanate was administered through the clergy of the Ulema, but the Ulema paid their allegiance to the supreme temporal power of a Turkish autocrat, of recent barbarian descent. Although the passing of the Sultanate within living memory has undoubtedly proved a setback to the Islamic faith, depriving it of its former administrative office, it still remains a spiritual if reactionary force in the Levant.

COMMUNISM
THE RELIGION OF THE FUTURE

In the modern world there can be little doubt that Communism holds the germ of a future religion, if it is not already an established gospel. It reproduces the typical revulsion against contemporary materialism and plutocracy that has been the main feature of the early phase of all great religions. Karl Marx is the Mahomet of this new faith: his Kapital its Koran; and Lenin the all-conquering Caliph Omar, who has gained an empire for the application of Communist dogma. Yet one can feel little sympathy with this new religion; it conveys little spiritual solace, and the conception of superorgamc reality is apparently denied to Communists, who recognize no supreme God. It is, however, possible that out of this unpromising material a real religion may yet be developed, as Islam had its origin in the robber-priest Mahomet, and Taoism was produced from the few obscure sayings of the philosopher Lau Tzi.

Before closing this discussion of the religious cycle, it is important to note that polytheistic tendencies may be traced in the further development of the religions of descendant as of original and offshoot civilizations, only in this case they are generally of a minor nature. The supreme God remains clearly dominant in the background, representing the ideal of superorganic unity despite the nationalist disruption of autocratic empire, but the local veneration of a regular pantheon of 'saints' gives an outlet for the forces of local patriotism. It is strange to find in two such highly developed religions as Buddhism and Christianity exactly similar methods of giving effect to local loyalties by means of 'saints,' 'relics,' etc., almost as if the one religion had been copying the other.

THE RELIGIOUS CYCLE

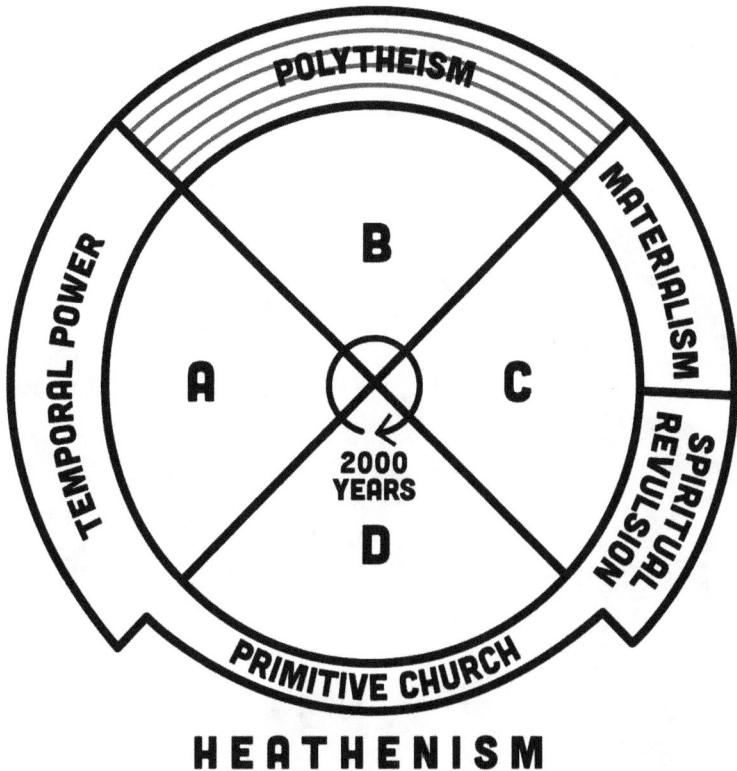

This is another form of cycle which throws a still more emphatic band of continuity across quadrant D, as a great religion is conceived in the democratic phase in quadrant C and persists through D to reach a culminating authority under autocratic auspices in quadrant A. The heathenism introduced by barbarian invasion has only a temporary effect in checking religious development, as the barbarians are soon converted to the established faith. The 'nadir' is clearly in the Materialist epoch of quadrant C, while the zenith is in quadrant A.

Chapter 8

The Artistic Cycle

In a general survey of the history of the development of art in the various regions of the earth the association between the great artistic epochs and the great religions of the world cannot fail to attract attention. There is clearly some intimate connection between the religious faith of mankind and the inspiration of its greatest artists. It is apparent that the same feeling of brotherhood in a great super-organic cause, that imbues the great mass of mankind with various religious beliefs, finds expression also through artistic genius in works of art raised to the glory of super-organic reality. While the multitude worships the higher being, which it constitutes, in its own dull, patient manner, the more gifted artist gives form to his belief in a higher destiny behind individual life by producing great artistic creations to the glorification of the supreme superman. As this is the case, we need not be surprised to find that artistic ability has waxed and waned with the general appreciation of the superorganic presence, which we term religion. Artists do not create works of art simply in order to gain a livelihood, as a shoemaker makes shoes, but rather abandon all opportunity of gaining a prosperous livelihood in order to create works of art. In this devotion to a higher duty they have more than a little in common with the earnest priest, who does not enter the ministry as a career of worldly ambition, but because he feels a higher call to direct his fellow-men to the service of supreme spiritual ideals. The priest and artist may not have always gone hand in hand, indeed there have been times when they have lived in the utmost enmity, but the really great eras of artistic accomplishment have been those when the artist and priest have felt the common origin of their inspiration in the superorganic godhead. Indeed, if we could gather all the great artistic treasures of the world from the dawn of history to the present day, we should find that the vast majority owe their existence directly or indirectly to religious inspiration.

We have found in our discussion of the religions of original and offshoot civilizations, that they were all centred upon the persons of original autocratic rulers, who had established civilizations out of chaos. Under these circumstances we need not be surprised that the early art of such original civilizations is primarily devoted to honour and glorify the supreme ruler himself be he Pharaoh, Minos, Son of

Heaven, Mikado, or Inca. Great monuments, tombs, and palaces, are constructed, and the artistic talent of the time engaged in their design and embellishment, all as a result of the inspiration of the communal veneration towards the divine autocrat.

In early Egyptian civilization the great Pyramids display not only the extraordinary self-sacrifice of the Egyptian people in an economic sense, expending the greater part of their excess energies in the erection of an entirely non-utilitarian structure purely as a religious monument to the divine Pharaoh, but also their belief in the pyramidal form as a perfect architectural design. Even in our own sophisticated age we cannot but be impressed by the massive grandeur expressed in the sheer simplicity of the Egyptian Pyramids. No subsequent age has possessed the self-restraint to produce a monument of such geometric austerity, and to this day no other mausoleum attains the impressiveness of these early Pyramids directing the thoughts of the onlooker towards the heavens above in one magnificent gesture of design. Although the Pyramids are generally ignored as works of art, no one can deny the magnificent rugged grandeur of the statues of the early Pharaohs of Memphis. A great awe and veneration of his subject obviously inspires the artist who attempts no slavish reproduction, but expresses by large surfaces and bold execution the awesome nature of the divine Pharaoh. Not men, but demigods, gaze down upon us from the Memphian monuments of this early epoch.

Of Minoan civilization we know comparatively little, but the magnificent palaces of Knossus show to what extent artistic talent was developed in the service of the autocratic Minos.

In China and Japan, the use of wood as the only building material in early times has deprived us of any permanent monument to the original art of either civilization; but the earliest examples of bronze work are reminiscent of early Egypt in their bold simplicity and grandeur of design.

In Peru, however, we find gigantic structures of masonry erected in honour of the state, and particularly of the divine Inca. Magnificent temples to the Sun and palaces of the Inca court vied with one another in splendour in the great central capital of Cusco.

We have seen that the great religions of history have their origin in the reaction against a decadent civilization in its last democratic phase, and survive a period of intercultural barbarism after the temporary collapse of culture to attain a height of authority in the succeeding cultural era.

The Artistic Cycle

This is equally true of art, and we find definite periods of artistic style, which coincide very largely with the great religions, and are obviously inspired by them. Exactly as in the case of the religions with which they are associated, such artistic epochs generally reach their peak of attainment in the early phase of the succeeding civilization, although clearly owing their origin to the culture of the foregoing era. We find it convenient, therefore, as a general rule, to associate these great artistic epochs with the later cultural era in which they reach their height, rather than with the foregoing in which they originated, and in doing this we are no doubt justified, for it would seem as in the case of the great religions that the new artistic style arising in the decadence of foregoing democracy anticipates the advent of the new as yet unborn superorganism of the future. The last democratic phase of a civilization is remarkable from an artistic point of view for the revolutionary break with the artistic tradition of the past, and the exploration of new lines of treatment.

The superorganism is gradually declining in this last phase of its existence, and the style which expresses its artistic personality loses authority in course of time, and can no longer control the natural idiosyncrasies of artistic genius. The individual artist no longer finds himself compelled to follow the traditional style of the past, but is at liberty to develop any style or form of artistic treatment which may appeal to him. The result is a rapid divergence of artistic forms, and a very grave decline of artistic ability as a whole. However, in course of time a new style of art crystallizes out of these many divergent forms under the inspiration of religion. This new style, although it may first develop in the last phase of a foregoing civilization, contains the germ of the artistic tradition of the new rejuvenated civilization to come. In modern Europe and America our democracies are today accompanied by grotesque experiments in new forms of artistic treatment and design, but it is still too early to point to any one of these many divergent schools, and state with any assurance that it alone holds the germ of future greatness. We can only wait patiently in this travail of the arts for the eventual birth of the style of the future. Could we detect it among its struggling competitors for public favour, we would no doubt be shocked by its apparent monstrosity.

When the democratic phase of foregoing civilization dissolves in complete disintegration into an intercultural barbarism, art, like religion, gains the veneration of the invading barbarians, and survives with an even greater intensity of inspiration to the time of cultural regeneration. Barbarism may be antagonistic to the actual material wealth and power of civilization, and overturn its most artistic

171

monuments in its brutal ignorance, but it has only respect for existing artistic ability, which it fosters in its own rude manner. Thus when dawning autocracy restores civilization as a superorganic reality, and cultural co-operation once more becomes a vital process, art surviving from earlier democracy is given an immense impetus of super-organic inspiration. Religion welcomes with an immense enthusiasm the advent of the newborn superbeing, and inspires art to lend its aid in glorifying the godhead. Hence we find in this period art closely allied to religion, when it attains its greatest triumphs in the service of the religious spirit of the time. Art expresses human emotions, and the sublime emotion of religious fervour must of necessity produce the finest examples of artistic creation.

Karnak

The Art of Ancient Egypt

In Egyptian art a very sharp break in continuity is perceptible at the time of the XII dynasty at Thebes. Monumental portraiture no longer shows signs of that divine grandeur that invests the earlier Pharaohs of Memphis; on the contrary, the Theban rulers appear as beings of mortal tissue, and in general a far greater naturalism is expressed in the artistic work of the time. The Hyksos barbarians, upon their invasion, adopted the Theban style as their own, and their kings frequently engraved their own names on the monuments of the earlier Pharaohs. Hence, when the XVIII dynasty expelled the Hyksos, they continued and developed the naturalism of Theban art. The unconventional freedom of style of the XII dynasty was crystallized into a vivacious style of somewhat romanticized but beautiful execution. The formalism of the early Memphian school is nowhere in evidence, and scenes of everyday life are frequently produced in every natural detail. It would, however, be a mistake to assume that this school of Egyptian art was occupied only with the pursuit of trivial natural effects; on the contrary, the finest examples of art in this period are to be found in the architecture and design of the temples of Ammon, where religious inspiration raised Egyptian art to sublime heights of accomplishment far above the mere reproduction of nature. It is impossible to give here any adequate description of Karnak at the height of its glory, with its avenues of huge pillars, pyloned gateways, towering obelisks; let it be sufficient to declare that no other period of art in history has produced a temple at once of such sublime proportions and yet so artistically designed. It was in the service of Ammon that Egyptian art was inspired to its greatest triumphs, and it was with the decline of Ammon as the religion of Egypt that Egyptian art degenerated to the poor imitations of later days.

Nineveh

The Art of Mesopotamia

In Mesopotamia we have already noted that the religion of Marduk never reached the height of authority that Ammon attained in Egypt, hence we find that art followed the temporal power from Babylon to Assyria, after the long-drawn barbarism of the Kassite period. It is to Nineveh, with its armed camp and magnificent palaces, that we must turn to find the finest examples of Mesopotamian art, which is entirely and strangely different from Egyptian art. While the Egyptians were splendid architects and sculptors in the round, they were generally weak in relief work, upon which they expended much ill-directed energy. On the other hand, at Nineveh, while architecture and sculpture lagged behind Egypt, relief panelling was developed to a much higher level. Indeed, one may actually assert that Assyrian relief work has never been surpassed in purely artistic design and decorative value, the frieze of the Parthenon itself not excepted. It is interesting to note that even the winged bulls and lions of Nineveh were not executed in the round, but formed a sort of block relief of a most peculiar and unparalleled design. In truth, the Assyrian craftsmen were the world's finest workers in relief, and subordinated all other forms of art to their supreme ability. Nineveh was the centre of a great artistic school inspired in the absence of a strong religious element in Mesopotamian civilization by the autocratic majesty of the Assyrian kings.

Asoka

The Art of Aryan India

In India, after the withdrawal of Alexander from the Punjab, the autocratic Maurya dynasty restored centralized government for the first time since the Aryans entered the country. The first Maurya kings maintained their position by resort to an immense military organization, and it was left to Asoka to adopt Buddhism as a means of enlisting public support for government. This enlightened autocrat extended the most liberal patronage to Buddhism, which found expression on the artistic side in the construction of many monuments and temples in honour of the Buddhist faith. Many thousands of pillars, the 'lats,' were erected throughout India, apparently to mark the spread of Buddhist conversion, and great buildings known as 'stupas' were constructed over places sacred to Buddha in northern India. These monuments and temples of the Buddhist religion show the recent evolution of architecture from an earlier time by the fact that, although constructed of stone, this stonework is treated in a most unusual manner, as if it were wood, imitation graining even being scored on its surface. Considering the discrepancy of style and material, the artistic work of Asoka's time shows a wonderful development of artistic talent. In particular, the 'torans' or carved gateposts of the 'stupas' are exceedingly beautiful, reproducing in the most elaborate forms of stone carving the primitive system of a horizontal bar of timber supported upon two similar uprights. So great has been the oriental admiration of these 'torans' that they have spread with Buddhism throughout the Far East, and are to be found as 'torii' in the greatest number in far-distant Japan. In the art of Aryan India we find again the inspiration of religion, for all artistic relics of this period are associated with the worship of Buddha.

We cannot leave the question of Buddhist inspiration of art here without noticing the magnificent architecture of pagodas and temples in those civilizations which have sprung from Aryan civilization in India. Ceylon and Burma are famous for their Buddhist architecture, temples being frequently of immense size. Towering pagodas and monumental figures of Buddha are to be seen on every side. Even in Java remains of Buddhist temples reveal the very high level of artistic accomplishment in the early epoch of Buddhist ascendancy in the archipelago.

GOTHIC

THE ART OF EUROPE

The style of architecture which owed its inspiration to the Christian religion has been termed Gothic, which is a most unfortunate misnomer, giving, as it does, a suggestion of barbaric origin. Actually an unbroken line of descent connects the 'Gothic' style with the civilized Roman architecture of the foregoing cultural era. This is fully recognized by Continental architects, who term the earliest Gothic 'Romanesque.' The round arches, circular ground plans, of the earliest Gothic are typical of the Roman love of the circle as the perfect curve, and were evolved long before the collapse of the Empire in the early Christian 'basilicas'; but here, as in many other similar schools of architecture which have been associated with religion, a wonderful dynamic development from early primitive forms has occurred as religion itself progressed as an idealist force. The early 'romanesque' forms still in use in the eleventh century were poor, primitive and uninspired as compared with the magnificent triumphs of the twelfth and thirteenth centuries, when the Church had risen to the supreme temporal power in Europe, and the Papacy was at the height of its autocratic authority. The great living power of inspiration behind the artists of this period is clearly to be seen in the uniformity of their style at any one epoch and its dynamic development of form from decade to decade. At no time did Gothic architecture become stereotyped or conventionalized; it was, on the contrary, dynamically alive, arising from primitive Roman sources, attaining a virile maturity, and declining into a sterile decoration. It possessed a real life-course as an organic form of artistic inspiration, and is today, and has been since the fifteenth century, as dead as Queen Anne. Gothic art was clearly a product of the great religious movement that placed the Papacy in absolute control of all Christendom, and should rather be termed Catholic than Gothic art.

MING

RECENT CHINESE ART

We have seen that in the case of Assyria, where the spiritual authority of Marduk at Babylon was weak in comparison with the temporal authority of the Assyrian royal house at Nineveh, art placed its services at the disposal of the stronger. In China a similar weakness of religion existed owing to the dual allegiance of the people to Buddhism and Taoism, and hence art was developed in the service of the Ming emperors after the expulsion of the Mongols rather than under the inspiration of religion. The Ming, after the first efforts leading to the defeat and subjection of the Mongols, relapsed into comparative political stagnation, but they nevertheless encouraged the restoration of Chinese art by an astoundingly generous patronage of contemporary artistic talent. We hear of one of the last of the Ming emperors actually ordering 96,000 pieces of porcelain for the use of the court in one year, and the monumental figures guarding the approach to the Ming tombs are reminiscent of the Egyptian honouring of dead emperors. Although, politically speaking, by no means an eminent dynasty, the Ming will live through history on account of the magnificent artistic work of their day.

Moslem

Levantine And Indian art

The democratic regime of the Caliphate in the Levant was marked by the development of art in an extreme sophistication of architectural forms. The simpler linear and circular outlines of the Greek and Roman styles were entirely abandoned in favour of experiments in curved outlines and surfaces of the most complex geometric design, which appealed strongly to the natural mathematical ability of the Mesopotamian peoples. Graduated and re-entering curves were adopted both in the outline of arches and the cross-section of domes and cupolas, in sharp contrast to the simple circular design of Roman arches and domes. Indeed, even Gothic architecture never approached the complication and sophistication of the curved outlines favoured by the Moslems, despite its elaboration of design. Islamic art may well be compared in this phase to the cubism of modern democratic art in its evolution of grotesque and even perverse forms of design, very different indeed from the classical austerity of Greece and Rome. In Mesopotamia the destruction of civilization upon the invasion of the Mongols was so complete that little of the art of the Caliphate survived, and on this account the semi-barbarian Turks, upon capturing Constantinople, turned to that city for artistic models. Hence in Levantine civilization Moslem art was stifled and had no opportunity of developing its great possibilities under the Turkish autocracy.

It is to India we must turn for the further progress of Islamic art. The Moslems from Mesopotamia conquered India a century or two before the advent of the Mongol barbarians from Central Asia, and managed to defend the country from Mongol invasion until the terrible Timur at last conquered Delhi and brought Moslem empire in India to an end. A century or so later, however, the Mogul Emperors themselves restored Indian culture, and gave a tremendous impetus to Moslem art, which reached its greatest height of perfection and sublime inspiration in their service. Tombs and palaces arose on the Indian plains, which are almost without a rival throughout the world in artistic beauty. Such buildings as the Taj Mahal rank with the best examples of any other style of architecture in the world, and show to what heights the art of Islam could rise under autocratic inspiration. It is indeed unfortunate that only in India did Moslem art survive barbarism to reach its culminating glory.

The Artistic Cycle

We have traced the main artistic sequence from its inception in the traditionless experimentalism of the democratic era through the 'Vandalism' of barbarian invasion to its culmination in the autocratic phase of a succeeding civilization, and have noted the essential association of this artistic sequence with the development of the great religions of mankind. One outstanding epoch of the cultural cycle has, however, remained untouched in this discussion, and an epoch that has produced many triumphs of artistic talent. Although Oligarchy falls outside the range of the main artistic sequence it cannot be neglected in a discussion of artistic style. We have seen that the religious faith of oligarchy is generally polytheistic or at least monotheism deeply tinged with the local loyalties of patriotism, as a result of the disruption of autocratic empire into a number of separate national states. Oligarchic art is similarly a matter of national or local schools, which differ very materially among themselves in subject and treatment, although conforming to one general style. These local schools have very frequently produced works of art even more beautiful and brilliantly executed than that of the best autocratic artists, but a certain instability and dependence upon individual masters of great personal talent prevent as a rule the establishment of a deep, lasting tradition of art, comparable with that of the main sequence. When the great master upon whom the local school depends for its inspiration is dead, the removal of his personal influence frequently brings the whole school to an abrupt end. Nevertheless there have been certain epochs in history when the disruption of artistic style into local schools under great masters of their craft has been productive of the most wonderful artistic work, which can rival the best autocratic art.

Greece immediately suggests itself as the outstanding example of oligarchic nationalist art of the very highest quality, far surpassing the cruder Cretan craftsmanship of the preceding autocratic era, and Greek influence spread over half the ancient world in a flood of Hellenism in the succeeding imperialist epoch.

Hindu art in India, although it could not rival the early Buddhist and later Mogul styles, was yet of very considerable merit in the many local schools of the disruptive Raja regime.

The varied styles of art in the Central American Maya and Aztec cities was by no means despicable.

In Europe itself, the Renaissance, although unfortunately hampered by its vain imitations of classical forms, yet produced some remarkable triumphs of sculpture and painting.

Oligarchic art may not possess the great superorganic inspiration of autocratic art, and may display a certain triviality, yet it has frequently reached the same level in sheer technical perfection of design and execution.

An interesting feature of artistic development, which occasionally introduces a disconcerting discontinuity into the evolution of artistic forms, is the occurrence of 'throw-backs' to earlier artistic models produced by former civilizations. These 'throwbacks' may conveniently be termed 'renaissance' epochs, from the typical case of the European revival of classical art in the recent nationalist era. The renaissance tendency is not, however, confined to the oligarchic phase of civilization, but may arise in any phase. The cause is generally to be sought in some strong revulsion against the immediate past, when the far-distant past is presented as an ideal state. A complete break with the art of the immediate past is followed by the imitation of early classical art with a greater or less degree of success. Naturally the result is a form of art, which being imitative lacks a certain vitality, but technical skill of the highest order is developed in reproducing classical originals and applying them to contemporary needs. The success of each renaissance era will depend very largely upon whether the classical period chosen for imitation is similar in super-organic phase to that of the later civilization. While a descendant oligarchic community will find suitable artistic inspiration in a previous oligarchic phase, it will not be able to adapt earlier autocratic and democratic forms so successfully to its purpose, and the same is true of the other cultural phases.

The earliest example of such Renaissance art is to be found in Egypt, where the unity of race throughout the Early and Late cultural eras encouraged the return to early sources of inspiration. The artists of the last democratic era of decadent Egyptian civilization, before its final submergence in the Mediterranean sphere of cultural influence, applied their energies to the reproduction of the weather-beaten originals of early Memphian autocracy, which they found about them in the newly restored metropolis. On account of the incongruous fact that a decadent democracy was looking for artistic inspiration in an early autocratic era, and because of the impossibility of the irreligious populace of the time rising to the ancient heights of religious fervour in which the Memphian monuments were conceived, this 'renaissance' was a dismal failure, and art in Egypt declined to a low level in this Egyptian 'Gotterdammerung.'

The European Renaissance is too well known to require any description. It was very much more successful than the Egyptian on account of the fact that the Lombard cities were able to recapture much of the original spirit of the Greek city states. The existence of a very similar social and political organization was exceedingly favourable to an understanding and reproduction of the classical art of Greece, and in architecture and sculpture the Italians were not unworthy of the task they had set themselves. Yet for all this affinity, imitation proved an insufficient basis for the inspiration of a great artistic style, and Renaissance art failed, except in the new technique of painting, to reach the high standard set by the Gothic craftsmen.

In China also a renaissance epoch may be traced when, following the expulsion of the Mongols, the artists of the Ming period turned to the bronzes of the earliest Shang era for models upon which to base a rejuvenation of Chinese art. Here one autocratic phase was looking for inspiration to another earlier autocracy, and on that account the attempt was strikingly successful. The Ming craftsmen were so apt in recapturing the inspiration of the early Shang artists that their work can often only be distinguished from that of the earliest times by the better workmanship of the later period. Such slavish imitations, however, placed a very severe limitation upon the contemporary development of art, and it is only in the art of porcelain manufacture, which was unknown to the early Shang regime, that we find the untrammelled evolution of a new virile style.

The last example of a form of renaissance was when the Turks, after their capture of Constantinople, actually turned to Byzantine originals for models for their mosques and palaces. This imitation of a foreign style of art was dictated by the fact that the Turks were at first cut off from Mesopotamian sources of inspiration by the Mongol posesssion of Bagdad; but the effort to inculcate a style, which was not only developed under very different social conditions but also by a people of entirely foreign culture, was doomed from the outset, and few artistic eras have been so poor and barren of inspiration as that of the Sultanate throughout the Levant. This bastard renaissance was a complete failure.

THE ARTISTIC CYCLE

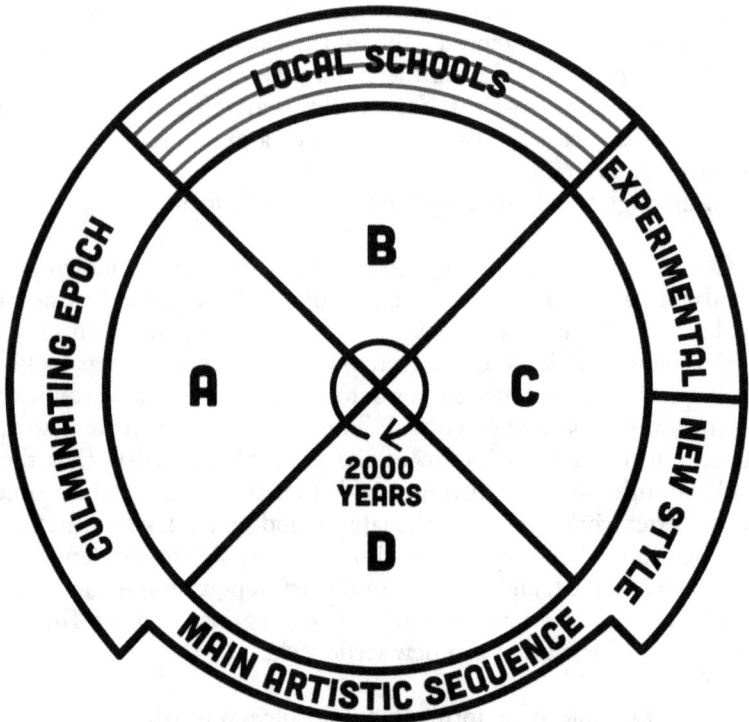

LOCAL SCHOOLS

CULMINATING EPOCH

EXPERIMENTAL

NEW STYLE

B

A

C

2000
YEARS

D

MAIN ARTISTIC SEQUENCE

VANDALISM

This cycle is obviously identical with the last in accordance with the evident association of art with religious inspiration. The 'nadir' of the artistic cycle, like that of the religious one, is without doubt situated in the early part of quadrant C. The 'zenith' of artistic talent is to be sought generally in quadrant A, but there have been cases of great artistic triumphs accomplished by the local schools of quadrant B, as, for example, in the classical age of Greece.

Chapter 9

The Relativity Of Morality

It is the purpose of this discussion to find in the cyclic repetition of cultural forms an indication of the superorganic nature of civilization. It is not only suggested that civilization may be compared by analogy with a natural organism: it is asserted that civilization is a natural, if super, organism. Civilization is the true 'superman' towards whom modern philosophy has been tending ever since Darwin propounded his principle of evolutionary advance in biology. It is only in the co-operation for a higher superorganic purpose that individual men become invested with the attributes of a 'superman.' Civilization is the result of human co-operation and is hence in itself the actual 'superman' whose immense powers are used by modern democracy for the enrichment and indulgence of the people. The conception of civilization as a superorganism is in itself not new; but the present discussion goes further when it applies the natural laws of growth and mortality to the superorganism. A living reality exists in civilization, a personality as vital and intense as that of any individual human being. This 'superman' is, however, no more immortal than is the human being. A civilization may persist for two thousand, even for three thousand, years, but a definite limit is set to its survival, as surely as the human being may not far exceed his allotted span of threescore years and ten. The greatest civilization must inevitably succumb in the fullness of time into an anarchic barbarism out of which a new rejuvenated culture will emerge.

The most striking proof of the presence of a 'superman' in civilization is to be found in religion, for the existence of a higher being on an exalted plane is an excellent explanation of the religious instinct in man, and the many religions of mankind, which remain perfect enigmas to modern materialism and scientific scepticism. We may not dismiss the great religions of the world, the most dynamic forces in history, as superstitious; and we must seek by all means possible an explanation of their great influence over mankind. Superorganic philosophy supplies such an explanation, and possesses on that account alone a very serious claim to consideration. Not only do the cultural cycles suggest an organic process of growth and decline, but the veneration for a higher being expressed by all civilized people at the height of their cultural attainment is a further and convincing argument for the reality of superorganic existence. In the enlightenment of modern scientific thought it is impossible to accept God as some vague intangible spirit resident in some unlocated heaven. Science wishes to collect, weigh, and test the properties of every 'spirit'; astronomy can find no trace of any 'heaven' in the depths of space. Religion must be rationalized if we are not to abandon it altogether with all its power for good and moral guidance. Superorganic philosophy effects this rationalization when it claims that the godhead venerated by the people of a civilization is in reality the superorganic personality which this civilization embodies.

There is no intention, however, in this identification of the godhead with the superorganism of degrading the source of religious veneration, but rather the desire of exalting the spirit of communal service, woefully weak in this democratic age, to the level of a supreme religion. Rationalization of the religious ideal must not bring religion into contempt; on the contrary, it must make it possible for the sceptical scientific thinkers of the present day to return to the religion of their forefathers with a fuller understanding of its hidden meaning.

As superorganic philosophy teaches the existence of a 'superman' in civilization, it follows as a matter of course that the only basis of morality must be found in the service of this superman by His constituent human units. Were it not for the existence of this higher being on an exalted plane far above human aspirations, it would be difficult indeed to find any other than a hedonistic basis for morality. In fact many philosophers of the past and present have arrived at a hedonistic creed from logical reasoning in the absence of any appreciation of superorganic reality, and modern democracy has gone very far in putting such a creed into practical effect. However, the presence of the superman in collective humanity enables us to escape from the egocentric arguments of the hedonists, which we could otherwise scarcely refute, and we find that the higher religious codes of such great spiritual leaders as Buddha and Christ have their full justification in superorganic fact. The superman has a paramount claim upon our services, for it is only through Him that we can attain to the highest expression of our possibilities. Communal service is the whole basis and foundation of morality, and this communal service must not be animated by any calculation of personal benefit. We must not think that if we do good to our neighbours they will in return do good to us. That form of communal service is entirely useless. We must serve the community even when the community demands some great sacrifice without any commensurate compensation. The superman in civilization is something outside ourselves, greater than ourselves, not simply the aggregate of all the little human beings that go to make up civilization, but a higher personality which commands our allegiance, veneration, and self-sacrifice. Throughout history mankind has dimly apprehended that self-sacrifice is greater and finer than self-indulgence; in the appreciation of superorganic reality lies a rational explanation of why this is essentially and inevitably the case. Just as the superman, civilization, is so much greater and more powerful than the human units of which He is composed, so are His interests more vital and important than those of the puny human individual.

Superorganic philosophy advances the service of the higher intrinsic spirit of civilization as the only true basis of morality, but this does not necessarily involve a simple permanent standard of ethics. If the superman were an immortal being, as conceived by Herbert Spencer and in less definite manner by H. G. Wells, then such a permanent code of morality might be evolved in His service, but we have found that civilizations no less than lower organisms are subject to the natural laws of growth and decline, are indeed as mortal as any other creatures. The service of such an ever-changing being cannot be codified to a simple standard on account of the differing conditions from epoch to epoch. We know that treatment suitable to a young child is inapplicable to a youth, and that exercise that builds up the muscles and strengthens the physique of a young man would be fatal to a man past middle age. The manner of service we render to the superorganism of which we are part must take into account the state of growth and development attained by our civilization.

Hence a special code of moral conduct must be adapted to each phase of civilization, and this ethical standard must be ever in flux to accommodate itself to the changing nature of the superorganism, which is the object of communal service. Morality is not absolute, but relative. The form of service best suited to further the aims of the superorganism will differ from epoch to epoch, and the moral code which is based upon this communal service must undergo similar changes. If we examine the moral codes which have commanded popular approval in the various phases of any civilization, we find that in greater or less degree these codes are adapted to the superorganic requirements of their time. Revolutionists would have us repudiate the doctrine that 'What is, is right,' but nevertheless each phase of civilization does evolve a moral code of its own best suited to its own particular requirements. Our forefathers were not absolutely wrong in their moral standards, which we repudiate so emphatically in our own time. They were relatively right in setting up a moral standard best suited to their conditions of cultural development, as we are relatively right in adapting an entirely different standard to our own. Einstein has shown us that the world of astronomical mechanics is really a four-dimensional continuum in which absolute motion exists, but that the motions we observe from our fixed position on the earth must remain because of our earthbound nature 'relative' three-dimensional projections of the true 'absolute' motions. Similarly the political and social world has an additional superorganic dimension imposed upon its human organization, and it is to this superorganic continuum that our code of morality must be referred. 'Absolute' morality exists on the superorganic plane in the service of the superorganism, but a 'relative' morality for each epoch of civilization will result from our earthbound point of view of the superorganism to which we belong.

If we follow the useful analogy of human growth as an illustration of superorganic development, we find that the active autocratic phase of civilization is equivalent to childhood in man. In a child all the natural processes are subordinated to the needs of growth. The body will tolerate no over-indulgence of any kind; the brain works along instinctive lines; the body is, in fact, completely disciplined in every part to its work of physical development. An autocracy applies a similar discipline to the community in the work of social and political growth; the individual is completely subordinated to the needs of the superorganism. Autocracy develops a complete moral code upon this basis, and it is in a sense in this moral code that the highest essence of the ideal of superorganic service is realized. Generally the moral standard of autocracy enjoys religious support. In Europe, for example, the Catholic Church presented its religious code of strict ecclesiastical discipline and service as the moral standard of the autocratic empire of Christendom. The moral code of the Catholic Church at that time may seem to us today a grievous tyranny, denying, as it did, personal freedom of speech and thought, condemning usury, and generally subordinating the individual and his interests to those of the Holy Church; but we must first appreciate the glorious reality of the Catholic Church at that time as a great spiritual and cultural force, before we can understand the basis upon which this moral code was founded.

The great organization of the Church, representing in most corporate fashion the superorganic nature of European civilization, was a vital and dominant force which naturally commanded the adherence, veneration, and service of the Christian community. We stand shocked today before the records of trials before the Inquisition, with their torture and terrible punishment, but the opinion of the time was convinced of the necessity of conserving the unity and glory of the Holy Church at all costs, even when the utmost inhumanity was involved. The superorganic or religious spirit of the Church was paramount, and the moral code of the time ruthlessly sacrificed the rebellious individual to the great superman so evidently in being.

Actually autocracy is a period of youth, and the strict discipline of the time that imposes a severe enforced form of service upon every individual does not necessarily involve the highest development of superorganic morality. As in human childhood, the moral standard of superorganic service is instinctive, that is, religious, and it is only in a conscious moral standard that the highest attainment of ethics can be reached. It is in the phase of oligarchy that this state is at least in part realized, for the disruption of autocracy modifies in a very large degree the former moral code of the complete subjection of individual interests to those of the superorganism. A section of the people becomes emancipated in the form of a privileged caste from direct enforced superorganic service, and is enabled to develop its cultural abilities in comparative freedom from material preoccupations supported by the lower orders. This privileged caste may be compared to the higher brain in man, which is emancipated from instinctive processes with the advent of maturity, and, drawing nourishment from the rest of the body, exists in parasitic freedom to think, conjecture, and philosophize. The higher 'brain' of society is the oligarchic caste which, requiring to take no heed for its subsistence, supported parasitically upon the labour of the common people, is enabled to establish purely cultural and philosophic schools of thought. Here is no enforced instinctive obedience to a strict moral code of superorganic service. The oligarchic caste is left in freedom to pass its life in idleness and luxury if it think fit. It has been emancipated by the superorganism in the hope of its producing great triumphs of philosophy and art, but it is not compelled to serve the higher aims of the superorganism. Yet every oligarchy on earth has at least in some measure realized its superorganic duty to the superman, and has voluntarily adopted a moral code of cultural service.

Throughout history it is to the oligarchic eras, and especially to disrupted nationalist periods, that we turn for philosophy, science, and general intellectual attainment. The city states of ancient Greece, the Contending States of ancient China, the national states of Europe, have supplied between them some nine-tenths of the purely intellectual, philosophical, and scientific genius of the whole world. It is to these eras that we owe such philosophic and scientific understanding of the world about us as we possess. These oligarchs have not wasted their privileged position in the pursuit of luxury and self-indulgence alone, they have also appreciated their moral duty of superorganic service to the cultural super-being. The code of law and custom that supported these oligarchic castes, and maintained them in a position of privilege over the common people, is condemned by modern democratic opinion, yet in its time it furthered the best interests of the superman by enabling a section of the community to turn from materialist preoccupations to the development of purely cultural and intellectual pursuits.

The democratic era in civilization is equivalent to old age in man. By the time a man has reached old age he may have amassed immense wealth and power, but the physical and mental virility of his youth is expended. His muscles, tissues, brain substance are still there in full possession of their faculties, but they no longer grant him the same efficient service as they did in his youth; on the contrary, they demand the most careful preservation and indulgence. This may not seem a very pleasant description of democracy to the democratic reader, but he must remember that we are not now dealing with democracy from the point of view of a democratic citizen, but from a purely superorganic point of view. It is a fact that cannot be avoided that democracy denies the existence of a superorganic godhead, and is determined to extract as much wealth and luxury as possible from civilization for the benefit of the individual citizens of the democratic community, while giving the least possible superorganic service in return, either in taxation, pure culture, or self-sacrifice of any kind. The state is regarded with the greatest misgivings by the democratic community and is deliberately reduced to the utmost impotence commensurate with the execution of democratic law and the maintenance of order. Yet even from the superorganic point of view, however much we may deplore the self-indulgence of democracy, we cannot offer any serious moral alternative. There can be no doubt that the superorganism is far gone in senile decay. The causes of this senility are as obscure to us mortals as our own senile decay and death. The fact remains that the superorganism is reduced to the feebleness of old age, and it is probably a physical impossibility for the human units of which this senile civilization is composed to bring about any rejuvenation of the old bones of the state by any communal action on their part. Under the circumstances it is clear that a new moral code will be evolved in which individual freedom and liberty will be the leading features. As the superorganism is no longer worth serving, unable indeed to profit in its senility from the service which may still be rendered it, the individual human units of the superman, not only a privileged caste but the whole community, are emancipated and liberated from cultural service to enjoy the accumulated fruits of the civilized control of nature, and to develop their own personalities free of all higher superorganic duties. The moral code of democracy, the 'liberte,' 'egalite,' 'fraternite,' with which democratic revolution has made us sufficiently well acquainted, is in its turn as true and relatively right as the previous codes of autocracy and oligarchy. The superman towards whom service is due has declined, and another basis of morality must be sought in the interests of the human individual himself. Democracy, the period of superorganic decline, is the era of individual prosperity. Let us make the most of this individualist paradise before civilization even in its materialist aspect perishes.

Now we approach an unpleasant subject, a subject especially unpleasant in these modern times. We have dealt with the moral codes of three of the four phases of the cultural cycle; we must now undertake to trace the moral basis of the fourth and last. Anarchy, as its name denotes, is equivalent to the death of civilization. Can there be such a thing as a moral code that advocates the extinction of civilization? There can be, is now, and has been in the past such a moral code. Democracy leads to a complete materialism during the decline of superorganic idealism, and this materialism rapidly develops into a plutocracy. At length a religious revulsion against the materialist nature of decadent civilization establishes a moral code, which opposes spiritual or communal ideals to the individualist materialism of the age, and actually advocates the destruction of existent civilization to make way for a new idealist system or 'heaven upon earth.' All the great religions of the world have started in this form, and Christianity is not least of these. The early Christians, and Jesus himself, were not reticent in foretelling the destruction of the existing plutocratic Romanized system of their day, and prophesying the coming of a new era of 'God's Kingdom upon Earth.' In superorganic language the coming civilization of the future is conceived, but its birth must involve the destruction of the parent to make place for its new rejuvenated vitality and growth. The moral code of the material destruction of civilization. on idealistic grounds has its basis in the service of the superorganism of the future, and the renunciation of the superorganism that has outlived its period of usefulness. The relativity of morality has reached its extreme of apparent perversity, and yet the absolute basis of superorganic service remains, even if the object of that service has been transferred from an old to a new still unborn cultural system.

Such is then the superorganic philosophy of history; the conception of civilization as a superman. I do not know how far the reader may find it of use in solving some of the problems of his own personal relations to the cosmos, and in understanding the inward meaning of historical movements in the past. I can only state that I personally have found in the tracing of this superorganic idea through the events of history and in the social and political forms of our own times the utmost satisfaction and a new appreciation of historical perspective.

The superorganic conception of history has seemed to shed a flood of illumination over so much that was obscure and inexplicable both in the historical narrative and contemporary social structure. It has seemed to reveal an underlying meaning beneath the bewildering diversity of human activities, and bind the whole complex structure into a united whole. More, it has restored in me a belief in the moral value and efficacy of religion, with an understanding of its real meaning.

I can only hope that a personal conception of cosmic reality, which has been of such great value to the writer in developing his attitude towards the problems of existence, will be of equal value to the reader in arriving at his own personal point of view.